Jamaica

Sarah Cameron & Ben Box

Credits

Footprint credits
Editor: Stephanie Rebello
Production and layout: Emma Bryers
Maps and cover: Kevin Feeney

Publisher: Patrick Dawson
Managing Editor: Felicity Laughton
Advertising: Elizabeth Taylor
Sales and marketing: Kirsty Holmes

Photography credits
Front cover: Norman Pogson/Shutterstock
Back cover: Carlos Gauna/Shutterstock

Printed and bound in the United States
of America

Publishing information
Footprint *Focus Jamaica*
1st edition
© Footprint Handbooks Ltd
September 2013

ISBN: 978 1 909268 33 3
CIP DATA: A catalogue record for this book
is available from the British Library

® Footprint Handbooks and the Footprint
mark are a registered trademark of
Footprint Handbooks Ltd

Published by Footprint
6 Riverside Court
Lower Bristol Road
Bath BA2 3DZ, UK
T +44 (0)1225 469141
F +44 (0)1225 469461
footprinttravelguides.com

Distributed in the USA by Globe Pequot
Press, Guilford, Connecticut

Every effort has been made to ensure that
the facts in this guidebook are accurate.
However, travellers should still obtain advice
from consulates, airlines, etc, about travel
and visa requirements before travelling.
The authors and publishers cannot accept
responsibility for any loss, injury or
inconvenience however caused.

The content of Footprint *Focus Jamaica*
is based on Footprint's *Caribbean Islands
Handbook*, which was researched and
written by Sarah Cameron.

Contents

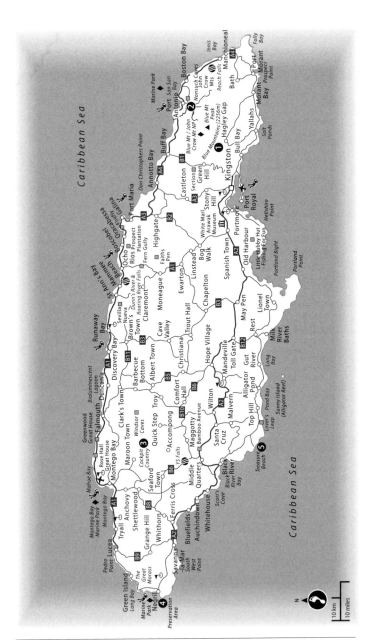

Jamaica has been called the Island of Springs. Xamayca, the name used by its pre-Columbian inhabitants, the Taínos, meant 'land of wood and water'. It is indeed an extravagantly beautiful island, with rolling hills and steep gullies and the spectacular Blue Mountains overlooking a coastline indented with bays and coves. Rain falls freely, water is abundant, the vegetation is luxuriant and colours vibrant. The people have a culture to match, from reggae and Rastafarianism to English plantation houses and cricket. The place lives and breathes rhythm: music is everywhere and Jamaica is a hub of creativity in the Caribbean. The cultural impact of reggae and its contemporary offshoot, dancehall, is now a global phenomenon.

Kingston is a busy capital city, the centre of commercial activity with a lively arts and entertainment scene including theatre, live music, clubs, bars and restaurants. It is where everything happens, albeit constrained and overshadowed by a reputation of gang-related crime and violence. Montego Bay is the tourist capital of the island, offering entertainment for holidaymakers in huge all-inclusive resorts or smaller hotels, whether they are wealthy celebrities seeking exclusivity in a boutique hotel or students looking for a good time on a budget. Every conceivable watersport is on offer in the resort areas on the north coast, where beaches are safe for swimming. The south coast, while having fewer beaches, is richly endowed with natural attractions such as Black River Safari and YS Falls and is fast becoming the destination for nature lovers and people wanting to get off the beaten track. Away from the coast you find the other Jamaica, of mountains and forests for birdwatching and hiking, rivers tumbling over boulders and small farms clinging to hillsides where the exquisite Blue Mountain coffee grows in the mist.

Planning your trip

Best time to visit Jamaica

As with everywhere in the Caribbean the climate is tropical. Jamaica is a mountainous, forested island and attracts more rain than its low-lying coral neighbours. The driest and coolest time of year is usually December to April, coinciding with the winter peak in tourism as snow birds escape to the sun. At this time, services are heavily booked in advance and prices are higher than the rest of the year. There can be showers in these months, but they keep things green. Temperatures then can fall to 20°C during the day, depending on altitude, but are normally in the high 20°s, tempered by cooling trade winds. The mean annual temperature is about 26°C. At other times of the year the temperature rises only slightly, but greater humidity can make it feel hotter if you are away from the coast, where the northeast trade winds are a cooling influence. Rain tends to fall in the afternoon and not for very long. This tourist low season, as well as being cheaper, is less crowded, but there may be some reduction in services. The main climate hazard is hurricane season (see box, page 8), which runs from June to November. Tropical storms can cause flooding and mudslides.

There are festivals and events the year round. See Festivals in Jamaica, page 14.

Getting to Jamaica

Air
There are three international airports: **Norman Manley** in Kingston (www.nmia.aero) and **Sangster International** in Montego Bay (www.mbjairport.com) for commercial flights and **Ian Fleming International** at Ocho Rios (www.ifia.aero), mostly for private aircraft.

Flights from UK British Airways (www.ba.com), Caribbean Airlines (www.caribbean-airlines.com) and **Air Jamaica** (www.airjamaica.com) fly from London, Gatwick to Kingston, while **British Airways**, **Caribbean Airlines** and **Virgin Atlantic** (www.virgin-atlantic.com) fly between Gatwick and Montego Bay. **Thomsonfly** (www.thomsonfly.com) also flies from Birmingham and Manchester to Montego Bay. There are lots of connections from other European cities.

Flights from the rest of Europe There are many charter flights from Europe which vary according to the season; check with a travel agent. **Arke Fly** (www.arkefly.nl) flies from Amsterdam, **Blue Panorama** (www.blue-panorama.it) and **Neos Air** (www.neosair.it) fly from Milan, **Condor** (www.condor.com) flies from Frankfurt, and **Jetair Fly** (www.jetair fly.com) flies from Brussels, all to Montego Bay.

Flights from North America Airlines flying between the US and Montego Bay are **Air Tran** (www.airtran.com) from Atlanta, Baltimore, Milwaukee and Orlando with connections to many other US cities; **Frontier** (www.flyfrontier.com) from Denver, Chicago and St Louis; **Sun Country Airlines** (www.suncountry.com) from Dallas/Fort Worth and Minneapolis/St Paul; **United** (www.united.com), principally out of Houston, but also Charlotte, Chicago, Newark and Washington; **US Airways** (www.usairways.com) with connections to many US cities, most via Charlotte and Philadelphia. **American** (www.aa.com) flies Miami-

Kingston and Montego Bay, also from Chicago and Dallas to Montego Bay. **Spirit Airlines** (www.spirit.com) from Fort Lauderdale to Kingston and Montego Bay; **Delta** (www.delta. com) to Montego Bay from Atlanta (also to Kingston), New York, Minneapolis/St Paul and Detroit; **Jet Blue** (www.jetblue.com) to Kingston from Fort Lauderdale and New York and to Montego Bay from Orlando, New York and Boston. Several airlines fly from Canadian cities to Montego Bay and, fewer, to Kingston: **Air Canada** (www.aircanada.com), **Air Transat** (www.airtransat.ca), **Sunwing Airlines** (www.flysunwing.com) and **West Jet** (www.westjet. com). **Caribbean Airlines** and **Air Jamaica** fly to several North American gateways (Fort Lauderdale, Miami, New York, Orlando, Toronto) and to various northern South American cities. **Fly Jamaica Airways** (www.fly-jamaica.com) flies from New York (JFK) to Kingston.

Flights from the Caribbean Regional airlines such as **Caribbean Airlines** and **Air Jamaica**, **Air Turks** and **Caicos** (www.airturksandcaicos.com) and **Cayman Airways** (www.caymanairways.com) have services to Kingston and/or Montego Bay from Antigua, Bahamas, Barbados, Grand Cayman, Grenada, Havana, Nassau, Port-au-Prince, Port of Spain, St Lucia, St Maarten, Santo Domingo, Tobago and the Turks and Caicos. **Copa** (www.copa air.com) fly to Latin America and some North American destinations via Panama City.

Airport information There are three international airports: **Norman Manley** in Kingston (www.nmia.aero) and **Sangster International** in Montego Bay (www.mbjairport.com) for commercial flights and **Ian Fleming International** at Ocho Rios (www.ifia.aero), mostly for private aircraft. Montego Bay airport is within walking distance of many hotels; from the others you will have to take transfers to hotels and resorts. From Norman Manley, which is best for the capital and Blue Mountain area, there is transportation to Kingston's domestic airstrip at **Tinson Pen**, 3 km from the centre of town on Marcus Garvey Drive, for national flights. Foreign exchange at Norman Manley and Sangster International Airports is handled by **Global Exchange** (www.globalexchange.com.jm). Excess Jamaican dollars may be changed back into US dollars on presentation of a receipt for the original purchase of the Jamaican dollars. The airports also have retail and duty-free shops, places to eat and drink and car hire facilities. Allow three hours to check in for a flight and go through all the security, baggage and documentation checks.

Sea

It is extremely difficult to book a passage by ship to other Caribbean islands. Throughout the year, at least a dozen cruise lines call at the ports of Falmouth (www. cruisefalmouthjamaica.com), Montego Bay (Freeport, www.cruisemontegobay.com), Ocho Rios or, less frequently, Port Antonio.

Hurricane season

June too soon, July stand by, August it must, September remember, October all over

In recent years there have been several late storms and the 'October all over' proved a myth. There was little hurricane activity in the region from the 1950s until the late 1980s. Many of the islands were not affected by hurricanes and residents thought little of them. Homes were not built to withstand severe storms. In 1989 this all started to change when several violent storms roared through the islands and Hurricane Hugo did untold damage in the US Virgin Islands. The next few years were relatively quiet but 1995 struck with a bang (three names were 'retired', never to be used again, in deference to the dead and injured) and was the start of a 10-year period that has gone down in history as the most active stretch on record for hurricanes. Analysts expect that this active hurricane era will last another two or three decades.

In the daily weather forecasts, a **tropical depression** is an organized system of clouds and thunderstorms with a defined circulation and maximum sustained winds of 38 mph (33 knots) or less; a **tropical storm** is an organized system of strong thunderstorms with a defined circulation and maximum sustained winds of 39 to 73 mph (34-63 knots); a **hurricane** is an intense tropical weather system with a well-defined circulation and maximum sustained winds of 74 mph (64 knots) or more.

A hurricane develops in warm waters and air, which is why the tropics are known for hurricanes. Powered by heat from the sea they are steered by the easterly trade winds and the temperate westerly winds, as well as their own ferocious energy. In the Atlantic, these storms form off the African coast and move west, developing as they come into warmer water. Around the core, winds grow to great velocity, generating violent seas. The process by which a disturbance forms and strengthens into a hurricane depends on at least three conditions: warm water, moisture and wind pattern near the ocean surface that spirals air inward. Bands of thunderstorms form and allow the air to warm further and rise higher into the atmosphere. If the winds at these higher levels are light, the structure remains intact and allows for further strengthening. If the winds are strong, they will shear off the top and stop the development. If the system develops, a definite eye is formed around which the most violent activity takes place; this is known as the eyewall. The centre of the eye is relatively calm. When the eye passes over land those on the ground are often misled that the hurricane is over; some even abandon safe shelter, not aware that as the eye passes the other side of the eyewall will produce violent winds and the other half of the hurricane. At the top of the eyewall (around 50,000 ft), most of the air is propelled outward, increasing the air's upward motion. Some of the air, however, moves inward and sinks into the eye and creates a cloud-free area.

The word 'hurricane' is derived from the Amerindian 'Hurakan', both the Carib god of evil and also one of the Maya creator gods who blew his breath across the chaotic water and brought forth dry land. In the north Atlantic, Gulf of Mexico, Caribbean and the eastern Pacific they are called hurricanes, in Australia, cyclones or 'willy willy', and in the Philippines, 'baguio'. In the Western North Pacific tropical cyclones of hurricane force are called typhoons. The first time hurricanes were named was by an Australian forecaster in the early 1900s who called them after political figures he disliked. During the Second World War US Army forecasters named storms after their girlfriends and wives. Between 1950-1952 they were given phonetic names (able, baker, charlie). In 1953 the Weather Bureau started giving them female names again. Today individual names (male and female) are chosen by the National Hurricane Center in Miami (www.nhc.noaa.gov) and submitted to the World Meteorology Organization in Geneva, Switzerland. If approved these become the official names for the upcoming hurricane season. As a system develops, it is assigned a name in alphabetical order from the official list.

There is very good information before hurricanes hit any land, thanks to accurate weather data gathered by the Hurricane Hunters from Keesler Airforce Base in the USA. During the storm season they operate out of St Croix in the US Virgin Islands, where they are closer to storms. This elite group of men and women actually fly through the eye of a hurricane in C130 airplanes gathering critical information on the wind speeds and directions and other data. This is sent to the Miami Hurricane Center where a forecast is made and sent to all islands in the potential path so they can prepare for the storm. Most of the island governments are now well prepared to cope with hurricanes and have disaster relief teams in place, while many of the island resorts, especially the larger ones, have their own generators and water supplies.

While a hurricane can certainly pose a threat to life, in most cases if precautions are taken the risks are reduced. Some of the main hazards are storm surge, heavy winds and rains. There is usually disruption of services such as communications, internal transport and airline services. Ideally, if a hurricane is approaching, it is better for the tourist to evacuate the island. During the hurricane, which is usually between six and 36 hours, you have to be shut up inside a closed area, often with little ventilation or light, which can be stressful. Some tourists think a hurricane will be 'fun' and want to remain on island to see the storm. This is not a good idea. If you do remain you should register with your local consulate or embassy and email home as soon as the warning is given to alert your family that communications may go down and that you will follow the rules of the emergency services. You should be prepared to be inconvenienced and to help out in the clearing up afterwards. Team work in the aftermath of a disaster can be tremendous.

When potentially violent weather is approaching, the local met office issues advisories:

Tropical storm watch be on alert for a storm (winds of 39-73 mph) which may pose threats to coastal areas within 36 hours.
Tropical storm warning the storm is expected within 24 hours.
Hurricane watch hurricane conditions could be coming in 36 hours.
Hurricane warning the hurricane is expected within 24 hours.

One of the best internet sites for information and data during an actual hurricane is www.stormcarib.com. The website of the Hurricane Hunters (www.hurricanehunters.com) has a virtual reality flight into the eye of a hurricane.

Jamaican geography

Jamaica lies some 145 km south of Cuba and a little over 160 km west of Haiti. With an area of 10,992 sq km, it is the third-largest island in the Greater Antilles. It is 235 km from east to west and 82 km from north to south at its widest, bounded by the Caribbean. Like other West Indian islands, it is an outcrop of a submerged mountain range. It is crossed by a spectacular range of mountains which rises to 2256 m at Blue Mountain Peak in the east and descends towards the west, with a series of spurs and forested gullies running north and south. The luxuriance of the vegetation is striking. Tropical beaches surround the island. The best are on the north and west coasts, though there are some good bathing places on the south coast too.

Boat information For visiting yachts there are three marinas: Errol Flynn Marina at Port Antonio (www.errolflynnmarina.com); the Montego Bay Yacht Club (www.mobayyachtclub.com) and the Royal Jamaica Yacht Club at Port Royal (www.rjyc.org.jm). See their websites for details of facilities and regulations.

Transport in Jamaica

Jamaica is not difficult to get around, but since there are few domestic flights, the only alternative is by road. Public buses are cheap, usually crowded and, outside cities, erratic. Allow plenty of time for the ride. Private transport for long journeys, either in the form of taxis or car rental, is expensive. For short journeys you can rent a scooter or bicycle.

Air
At the time of writing the only scheduled domestic flights were between Montego Bay and Negril with **International AirLink** (www.intlairlink.net), US$118 per person one way. They also have charter services between the main domestic airports: **Tinson Pen Aerodrome** in Kingston, **Ian Flemming International** at Ocho Rios, Negril Aerodrome and **Ken Jones Aerodrome** at Port Antonio.

Road
Highway 2000 is a four- to six-lane toll road (speed limit 110 kmph, tolls from US$0.70-3) connecting Kingston and Mandeville and eventually Montego Bay, and Kingston and Ocho Rios. The first stage from Kingston to Williamsfield (beyond May Pen) has been built and the northern link to Ocho Rios has been started. There is a Northern Coastal Highway from Negril through Montego Bay, Falmouth and Ocho Rios to Port Antonio. Other roads are often poorly lit, twisty and potholed, especially in mountainous areas, where there are no guard rails. The speed limit is 80 kmph in unrestricted areas and 50 kmph or less in townships and other built-up areas. Try to avoid driving outside towns at night. Plan ahead because it gets dark early. Traffic congestion is to be expected in all large towns and jams are the norm in rush hour. Distances and journey times of major routes: Kingston to Montego Bay 193 km (3½ hours), to Ocho Rios 86 km (two hours), to Port Antonio 98 km (two hours); Montego Bay to Negril 76 km (1¼ hours), to Ocho Rios 102 km (1¾ hours); Ocho Rios to Port Antonio 196 km (1¾ hours); Negril to Treasure Beach 97 km (2 hours).

Bus Public road transport is mostly by minibus. Always take a bus with a red **PPV** (Public Passenger Vehicle) licence plate. Some tourist areas are served by shuttle buses, but to get to other areas you should go to city bus terminals and find out which bus or route taxi goes to your destination. Luxury bus services are run by **Knutsford Express** (www.knutsfordexpress.com) from Kingston to Falmouth, Mandeville, Montego Bay, Negril, Ocho Rios, Santa Cruz and Savanna La Mar and between these towns. In the Kingston area buses are run by the **Jamaican Urban Transit Company** (JUTC, www.jutc.com), whose fares range from US$0.80 for a standard ticket to US$2.45 on premium express routes. The **Ministry of Transport, Works and Housing** (www.mtw.gov.jm) has information on public transport, roadworks and related matters.

Car/car hire Undoubtedly a rented car is the most satisfactory, and most expensive, way of getting about. All the major car rental firms are represented both at the airports and in the major resort areas. There are also numerous local car rental firms which are mostly just as good and tend to be cheaper. The tourist board has a list of members of the **Jamaica U-Drive Association** (JUDA) ① *31 Hope Rd, Kingston 10, T9202872, www.rentacarja.com*. The Association's website also gives a full list of all its members. In high season be prepared to pay considerably more than in North America or Europe. In low season rates are greatly reduced. A small economy car costs US$90-100 per day to rent in high season, compared with US$38-40 in low season (US$540-600 and US$225-235 per week respectively). A mid-sized car is US$110 (US$660 a week) high season, US$45 (US$270) in low season. A large vehicle is US$130 (US$780 high season, US$70 (US$420) low. CDW is not included and rates vary with size of car. Tax of 16.5% is not included either. Many companies operate a three-day minimum hire policy. Clients must be over 21 years old and have had a valid driver's licence for a minimum of a year. A surcharge may be imposed on drivers aged 21 to 25. A North American driving licence is valid for up to three months per visit, a British licence 12 months and a Japanese licence one month. **Remember to drive on the left**. Breath tests for drunk driving and speed traps are enforced. Most petrol/gas stations are open on Sunday. There are few 24-hour stations, but most close at 2200.

Taxi There are taxis, with red **PPV** (Public Passenger Vehicle) licence plates, in all the major resort areas and at the airports. Some have meters, most do not. The important point is to find out the fare before you get in and then agree the fare with the driver before setting out. The police are a good source of information on fares, as are tourist information centres. Fares vary from town to town, but a short ride in Negril for instance, will cost about US$5. There is usually a night-time surcharge. Taxis charge about US$60 from Norman Manley airport to hotels in New Kingston and from US$30 from Montego Bay airport to local hotels. Taxis licensed to a hotel will charge more than a taxi on the street. 'Route taxis' operate like minibuses, that is, they have a set route and can be flagged down at the bus stop or anywhere along their route, which is displayed. They will carry up to four passengers and charge about US$1 per person. Avoid overcrowded vehicles as they may be stopped by the police for road code violations; a clean and well-maintained vehicle says volumes about the operator and the likelihood of having a safe and comfortable trip. Another option is go with one of the special tourist transfer companies like **JUTA** (Jamaica Union of Travellers Association, www.jutatoursltd.com) or **JCal** (www.jcaltours.com), which have comfortable vehicles between airports and resorts and run tours.

Maps The *Discover Jamaica* road map (American Map Corporation) is widely available free from tourist offices. It has plans of Kingston, Montego Bay, Negril, Mandeville, Ocho Rios, Port Antonio and Spanish Town. Good clear series of 1:50,000 maps covering Jamaica in 20 sheets from Survey Department, National Land Agency, 23½ Charles St, Kingston, T922 4278. Available from booksellers are the maps by ITMB (*Jamaica & the Cayman Islands*, 1:250,000 & 1:37,500, with town plans, www.itmb.ca), Reise Know-How (1:150,000, www.reise-know-how.de) and Shell (1:250,000, with town plans, www.macmillan-caribbean.com).

Where to stay in Jamaica

There are hotels and guesthouses all over Jamaica, with the greatest concentration of hotels around the coast and most of those on the north coast. Inland you find smaller, more intimate places to stay. Aim to arrive at Montego Bay rather than Kingston because the former is the island's tourism capital with a greater variety of affordable accommodation. Kingston is more geared towards the business traveller market. However, if you can arrange to fly out from Kingston you will have a chance to get the flavour of the Jamaican experience in both cities. Get hold of the tourist board's list of hotels and guesthouses offering rates and addresses, and also a copy of **Jamaica Vacation Guide** (both free). All-inclusive resorts were invented in Jamaica and are extremely popular. They are mainly along the north coast; some allow children but most are for couples only. As with any all-inclusive hotel, you get what you pay for and a cheap deal will probably mean limited quality.

The **Jamaica Association of Villas and Apartments (JAVA)** ① *Shop No 4, Ocean Village Shopping Centre, Main St, Ocho Rios, Box 298, T9742508, www.javavillas.org*, represents over 300 private houses, villas and apartments. Renting a **villa** (see also ① *www.villasin jamaica.com*) may be an attractive option if you do not intend to do much travelling and there are four to six of you to share the costs (starting at about US$2500 per week for a nice villa with private swimming pool and fully staffed). You will, however, probably have to rent a car as you will have to take the cook shopping, etc. You can go even more upmarket and pay up to US$16,000 a week for a fully staffed luxury villa.

Food and drink in Jamaica

Food
Jamaican food is spicy and aromatic while also heavy on the carbohydrates and tending to be greasy. Imported African slaves brought many of their traditional foodstuffs with them and when they were working in the fields they needed lots of starchy foods to give them energy, now known as 'ground provisions' or 'food'. The bountiful land gave them lots of variety and Jamaican cuisine now also encompasses influences from Britain and later immigrants from Europe and Asia as well as from the indigenous Taínos who inhabited the island before they all arrived. There are many unusual and delicious vegetables such as cho-cho (christophene or chayote), callaloo and breadfruit, and fruits such as sweetsop, soursop, star apple, guinep and naseberry (sapodilla). National specialities include saltfish (salt cod) and ackee, saltfish fritters and curried goat. Ackee is a national delicacy, but not to every foreigner's taste. Although treated as a vegetable, it is a red-skinned fruit from a tree, which can only be eaten after the pod opens; before that it is poisonous. It is cooked with onions and peppers and served with saltfish, often also with roasted breadfruit, boiled green bananas, fried plantains or bammies for a hearty breakfast.

Price codes

Where to stay
$$$$ over US$150 $$$ US$66-150
$$ US$30-65 $ under US$30
Price of a double room in high season, including taxes.

Restaurants
$$$ over US$12 $$ US$7-12 $ US$6 and under
Prices for a two-course meal for one person, excluding drinks or service charge.

Jerked pork is highly spiced pork which has been cooked in the earth covered by wood and burning coals. Chicken is cooked in the same way. Watch out for the scotch bonnet chillies which will give you an instant suntan. Festival is a very popular finger-shaped cornmeal dough usually eaten with fried fish. Bammy is pancake-shaped cassava bread, fried, grilled or steamed, also usually eaten with fried fish. Patties, sold in specialist shops and bars, are seasoned meat, vegetables or lobster in pastry, and very good value. Curried lobster is a delightful local speciality. The closed season for lobster fishing is April to June, so if lobster is on the menu during those months check where it has come from. Stew peas is chunks of beef stewed with kidney beans and spices and served with rice. Run down (run-dong) is salted mackerel stewed in coconut milk, tomatoes, onions and peppers, served with boiled green bananas, yams and boiled dumplings. Escoveitch fish is prepared by marinating whole fried fish in vinegar, onions, cho-cho, carrots and hot peppers, eaten hot or cold. Along the coast, fish tea is a hotch potch of the day's catch made into a soup, sold by the cup, while 'mannish water' is goat's head soup. Jamaicans tend to 'marry' one food item to another and being able to order the appropriate combination from the menu is to demonstrate a mastery of local cuisine.

While travelling around the island you will come across roadside stalls selling local snack food. These may just be patties, which you can wash down with a beer. Some, however, have developed into regional specialities and Jamaicans drive miles to eat there. Boston Bay, for instance, is famous for its jerk meats, where you'll find huge barbecues made of oil drums and the air is full of the pungent smell of chicken, pimento and hot peppers. In the Black River area, tiny peppered shrimps are offered at the roadside, sold in bags for snacking on.

Drink

Local rum is combined with local fruit juices to create cocktails, or mixed with *Ting*, a local carbonated grapefruit soft drink. *Red Stripe* lager, with which, the locals say, no other beer compares, is about US$1.50 at a roadside bar, considerably more in a hotel. If you want any other beer you will have to specify the brand, otherwise you will automatically be given Red Stripe. *Irish Moss* is made from red algae mixed with herbs and roots and considered an aphrodisiac. All rums are very cheap duty free.

Eating out

The best restaurants offer international cuisine, making the most of local ingredients as well as imported specialities. You can find a restaurant for practically any nationality in

Jamaica: Mexican, Italian, French, Chinese, fusion, and there are hundreds of good places to eat. Jamaicans tend to eat local dishes for lunch or snacks and at home, while a beach barbecue will be a variety of fish with local accompaniments or jerk meats. In Kingston there are many restaurants designed for the business market, but there are also many casual places for trend-setters: sports bars, music venues and themed restaurants. Sports celebrities such as Usain Bolt and Courtney Walsh have their own restaurants and bars. See www.eatoutjamaica.com for a database of places to eat, from bakeries to gourmet restaurants, all round the island.

Festivals in Jamaica

The tourist board publishes a calendar of events which covers arts and sports festivals, **www.jamaicatravel.com**. Cultural events are organized by the **Jamaica Cultural Development Commission (JCDC)** ① *3-5 Phoenix Av, Kingston 10, T926 5726, www.jcdc.gov.jm*. They publish a full calendar of national and local cultural events. See also **www.keepitjiggy.com**, which has a calendar of events.

Jan New Year's Day. Rebel Salute (www.rebelsaluteja.com) is held mid-Jan, organized by reggae stalwart and Rastafarian, Tony Rebel. In 2013 it was held at Richmond Estate, Priory, St Ann. It features live performances by legendary reggae musicians and is patronized by a wide cross-section of Jamaicans who come together to enjoy the sounds of the 1970s and 1980s. The grounds become a huge encampment when fans descend from home and abroad. Jamaica Jazz and Blues Festival, Greenfield, Trelawny (www.jamaicajazzandblues.com) is held at the end of the month, attracting many international stars.

Feb Feb is Reggae Month, to coincide with Bob Marley's earthday (birthday) on 6 Feb. On this date **Bob Marley Day** is celebrated at the Bob Marley Museum, Kingston, and several other locations. **Fi Wi Sinting**, Portland's Heritage Fest is held at Somerset Falls, Hope Bay, Portland (16 Feb 2014), and features some of the best of local cultural traditions in food, crafts, poetry, music and dance, including folk forms such as Kumina, Nyabinghi drumming, Mento and other rhythms. It is organized by Sister P (Pauline Petinaud, T715 3529, www.fiwisinting.com), a cultural icon in the parish, who promotes authentic Jamaican culture through the lives of ordinary people.

Feb-Apr Carnival or Bacchanal (www.bacchanaljamaica.com) is celebrated with events that start in Feb and continue to Apr, at various locations around the island, attended by thousands. Parades are made up of different groups in costumes, marching and dancing for the whole day through the streets. Upon reaching their destination there is a competition between the different groups, judged on stage according to their energy, creativeness and design. You can choose to be a part of the competition, by dressing in the costumes of a particular group, or you can simply march along with them in regular clothes as a supporter.

Mar Misty Bliss (www.blueandjohncrow mountains.org) is an annual cultural event held on the last Sun in Mar at Holywell Park in the Blue Mountains, with live entertainment, traditional Jamaican food and authentic craft markets.

Mar/Apr Ash Wed, Good Fri, Easter Sun, Easter Mon are all local holidays when everyone on the island goes to church and congregations spill out on to the streets. Over the Easter weekend the **Montego Bay Yacht Club** holds its **annual regatta**. In Apr the popular **Trelawny Yam Festival** is held in Albert Town, Trelawny.

May Calabash Literary Festival, www.calabashfestival.org, includes literary

Lightning Bolt

Who has not yet heard of Usain 'Lightning' Bolt, the fastest sprinter on the planet and star of the 2012 London Olympics? Bolt was the youngest ever world champion when he won gold in the 200 m in the 2002 World Junior Championships in Kingston. At age 15 he already stood 6' 5" tall (1.96 m), but didn't take himself or his running very seriously, causing trouble on many occasions for his trainer/coach. In 2003 he claimed one of the five IAAF Rising Star Awards given to the world's most impressive junior athletes and moved from Trelawny, where he'd been running since primary school, to Kingston, to participate in the IAAF's High Performance Programme. Every talent spotter's dream, he has fulfilled and probably exceeded their expectations.

Bolt now holds the world record in both the 100-m and the 200-m sprint as well as being part of the team to hold the 4 x 100-m relay record. He is the reigning Olympic champion in these three events, the first to win six Olympic gold medals for sprinting, eight times world champion and the first to win the double triple, having won the 100 m, 200 m and 4 x 100 m in both the 2008 and 2012 Olympics. He won all three again in the 2013 World Championships in Athletics, while his compatriot, Shelly-Ann Fraser-Pryce won all three in the women's events. Bolt is the most successful athlete in the 30-year history of the Championships, the highest paid athlete ever in track and field, and also the most marketable. You can't miss him.

performances by top local and overseas artistes over a 3-day weekend at the end of May in Treasure Beach. There are also live post-show musical performances on each night. Events leading up to the festival are held in Kingston, with film festivals and workshops. Calabash was founded in 2001 by the novelist Colin Channer and is the only international literary festival in the English-speaking Caribbean. The event was not held in 2013; check the website for 2014.

23 May Labour Day, a local holiday when you can find various activities.

Jun Jamaica International Jazz Festival is based in Ocho Rios, but there are events elsewhere on the island (www.ochorios jazz.com). Concert and workshops take place over a week in the middle of the month.

Jul Reggae Sumfest, www.reggaesum fest.com, runs for a week and is possibly the greatest reggae show on earth. Certainly Jamaica's leading annual reggae music festival, at Catherine Hall Entertainment Complex in Montego Bay, it attracts all the most popular musicians from Jamaica and

overseas, with each night themed according to types of artistes performing. The Portland Jerk Festival is held in the 1st week of Jul, bringing lovers of spicy food from all over the island to enjoy finger-licking pork, chicken, fish and more. For a different type of food festival, there is the Little Ochi Seafood Carnival at Little Ochie, Alligator Pond, Manchester, in the middle of Jul.

Aug The celebrations around Emancipation Day, 1 Aug, and Independence Day, 6 Aug, last a week, ending with a street dance at Half Way Tree. Jamaica International Reggae Film Festival (www.reggaefilm festival.com) is held at Island Village, Ocho Rios on 1-5 Aug. Films, documentaries and music videos are shown. It ends with an awards ceremony. Also at the beginning of the month (1-6 Aug) is the Smirnoff Dream Weekend (www.jamaicadreamweekend. com), a music festival in Negril, with concerts, raves and parties.

Oct The weekend leading up to National Heroes Day (3rd Mon in Oct) is packed with parties on the north coast and crowds of

Cricket in the Caribbean

Cricket in the Caribbean is a game played to a backdrop of rapturous music, stomach-tingling food, fervent politics and joyous partying. It is played in front of the most knowledgeable spectators in the world, who will stop you in the street to provide a breakdown of tactics and techniques (or their absence) in West Indian batting. It is played in the sun (mostly). It is played to laughter.

The six first-class teams are: Jamaica, Trinidad and Tobago, Barbados, Guyana, Windward Islands and Leeward Islands. Inter-island matches are hugely entertaining, with a one-day competition before Christmas and the four-day Regional Four Day Competition from January to March. Unless the West Indies side is on tour, all the international players are required to play in the competition, so the standard is high. Consult www.caribbeancricket.com, www.windiescricket.com, or www.cricinfo.com.

The West Indies hosted the six-week **Cricket World Cup** in 2007, with matches played in Antigua and Barbuda, Barbados, Grenada, Guyana, Jamaica, St Kitts and Nevis, St Lucia and Trinidad and Tobago, while warm-up matches were also played in St Vincent. All these islands now have superb facilities with totally new or completely refurbished grounds and there is a wealth of choice of venues for Test Matches, One-Day Internationals or other world-class cricket.

The development of cricket and of the West Indies team in the English-speaking Caribbean during the 20th century reflected the political struggle for Independence. The best cricketers became respected role models. Learie Constantine, a barrister and advocate of cricketers' rights, paved the way in the 1920s and 1930s. Lightning fast bowler, cavalier batsman, the finest fielder in the world, he was loved and revered from Trinidad to England. He captained the Dominions cricket team that played against England in the series immediately following The Second World War; a massive recognition at that stage of the 20th century for a black man in a white-dominated team.

The great Jamaican batsman, George Headley, became the first black person to captain the West Indies side in 1948. He paved the way for Frank Worrell, another believer in players' rights, who was the first fully appointed black captain of the West Indies a decade later. The first West Indies win in England brought joyous acclaim in 1950 and new respect in the English-speaking world. Worrell, with his two seminal series as captain in Australia in 1960-1961 and England in 1963, brought a unity to the Caribbean and a consistency to the team that lasted for over 35 years. Sir Garry Sobers remains arguably the greatest cricketer yet born. The dominance of Clive Lloyd and Viv Richards in the 1970s and '80s, both in batting and captaincy, took the West Indies to a new level. The bowling of Roberts, Garner, Holding, Marshall, Ambrose and Walsh struck both fear and admiration into many an armchair spectator, let alone the batsmen who faced them. For over a decade, West Indies cricket has been in decline. Only the batting brilliance of Brian Lara kept the side from complete annihilation but he retired in 2007 after the World Cup. The team's most recent success was to win the ICC World Twenty20 Championship in 2012.

In Jamaica the game is represented by the Jamaica Cricket Association (JCA), George Headley Stand, Sabina Park, Kingston, T9670322, www.cricketjamaica.org.

people gather from all over the island for non-stop partying, day and night.

25-26 Dec Christmas Day, Boxing Day. **Sting** is held on Boxing Day at the Jamworld Entertainment Centre, Portmore, St Catherine. It is the grand finale of dancehall acts for the year, a meeting place for the top artists of the genre. There are usually many other festivals and craft fairs in the period leading up to **New Year's Day**.

Essentials A-Z

Accident and emergency
The universal emergency number of 911 has been adopted, but not as the exclusive number. The Jamaica Constabulary Force (www.jcf.gov.jm) can still be contacted in an emergency on 119, and the Jamaica Fire Brigade (www.jamaicafirebrigade.org) on 110.

Children
Several exclusive resorts on Jamaica limit the age of children allowed. Some of the all-inclusive resorts are geared towards couples and therefore kids are not accepted. At the cheaper end of the market there will be no restrictions. In the resort hotels there is a standard reduction for children or they go free if sharing a room with 2 adults. Several hotels offer kids' clubs which amuse the children all day and allow adults to go off and do their own thing. Babysitting services are usually available.

Food is not usually a problem as burgers, pizza, pasta or chicken and chips are available for fussy eaters. Bananas and avocados are safe, easy to eat and nutritious; they can be fed to young babies and most older children like them too. Buy what you can when you see it from farmers at the market or roadside stalls. If you are not in self-catering accommodation, there are many hotels with a kitchenette in the room so you can prepare snacks or light meals to fill a nagging hole. In restaurants you can ask for children's portions or divide 1 full-size helping between 2 children. It is advisable to take all your own baby food and nappies/diapers if travelling with babies, as you cannot rely on your regular brand being available.

Clothing
Light summer clothing is needed all year round and up in the mountains, with a sweater for cooler evenings. Some hotels expect casual evening wear in their dining rooms and nightclubs, but for the most part dress is informal. Bathing costumes, though, are only appropriate by the pool or on the beach.

Customs and duty free
Tourists over 18 may bring in to Jamaica 200 cigarettes or 50 cigars or ½ lb of other tobacco products; 2 litres of alcohol; a reasonable amount of personal and household effects. There are no restrictions on the export of tobacco products and alcoholic beverages.

Drugs
Marijuana (*ganja*) is widely grown in remote areas and frequently offered to tourists. In some cases tourists have been threatened for refusing to buy drugs. Cocaine (not indigenous to Jamaica) is also peddled. Possession of either drug is a criminal offence. On average over 200 foreigners are serving prison sentences in Jamaica at any given time for drug offences. The police stop taxis, cars, etc, in random road checks. Airport security is tight with sniffer dogs and scans.

Electricity
Voltage in Jamaica is 110 volts, 50 cycles AC; some hotels have 220 volts. Plugs or electric sockets are twin, flat-pinned, as in the US and Canada.

Embassies and consulates
For embassies and consulates of Jamaica, see www.embassy.goabroad.com.

LGBT (lesbian, gay, bisexual and transgendered)
There has been a gradual acceptance of LGBT travellers in the Caribbean in recent years, partly in response to the power of the tourist dollar. Jamaica, however, is not seen as a destination for LGBT tourists and Jamaican law contains prohibitions of certain sexual practices between men. See the US State Department's travel advisory

for the country: www.travel.state.gov/travel/cis_pa_tw/cis/cis_1147.html. Although the law does not include women in its prohibitions, in public perception same-sex relationships between women are generally not tolerated. The homophobic content of the lyrics of some of the major music artistes and violence towards Jamaican gays receives some adverse publicity (mostly abroad), but attitudes are slow to change. The Jamaican Forum for Lesbians, All-Sexuals and Gays (J-FLAG) documents these activities and presses for change. See www.jflag.org. A few small hotels cater for foreign LGBT guests and it would appear that their privacy is respected, but advice is to be aware of the overriding anti-gay climate.

Health

In general, health care is good with average life expectancy of 75 years. Declining government spending on health and social programmes has led to falling standards and a rise in private hospitals and clinics with rising costs. The best public health institutions are in Kingston and Montego Bay.

See your GP or travel clinic at least 6 weeks before departure for general advice on travel risks and vaccinations. Try phoning a specialist travel clinic if your own doctor is unfamiliar with health in the region. Make sure you have sufficient medical travel insurance, get a dental check, know your own blood group and, if you suffer a long-term condition such as diabetes or epilepsy, obtain a **Medic Alert** bracelet (www.medicalert.org.uk).

The major risks posed in the region are those caused by insect disease carriers such as mosquitoes and sandflies. The key parasitic and viral diseases are malaria and dengue fever. The occurrence of **malaria** is reported as very low in Jamaica and advice is to investigate fever promptly, rather than take prophylaxis. **Dengue fever** is particularly hard to protect against as the mosquitoes can bite throughout the day as well as night (unlike those that carry malaria); try to wear clothes that cover arms and legs and also use effective mosquito repellent. Mosquito nets dipped in permethrin provide a good physical and chemical barrier at night.

Some form of **diarrhoea** or intestinal upset is almost inevitable, the standard advice is always to wash your hands before eating and to be careful with drinking water and ice. In a restaurant buy bottled water or ask where the water has come from. Food can also pose a problem, be wary of salads if you don't know whether they have been washed or not.

There is a constant threat of **tuberculosis** (TB) and although the BCG vaccine is available, it is still not guaranteed protection. It is best to avoid unpasteurized dairy products and try not to let people cough and splutter all over you.

Websites

www.cdc.gov Centres for Disease Control and Prevention (USA).
www.nhs.uk/nhsengland/Healthcare abroad/pages/Healthcareabroad.aspx Department of Health advice for travellers.
www.fitfortravel.scot.nhs.uk Fit for Travel (UK), a site from Scotland providing a quick A-Z of vaccine and travel health advice requirements for each country.
www.itg.be Prince Leopold Institute for Tropical Medicine.
www.nathnac.org National Travel Health Network and Centre (NaTHNaC).
www.who.int World Health Organisation.

Insurance

Take out some form of travel and health insurance, wherever you're travelling from and to. This should cover you for theft or loss of possessions and money, the cost of medical and dental treatment, cancellation of flights, delays in travel arrangements, accidents, missed departures, lost baggage, lost passport and personal liability and legal expenses. Also check on the inclusion of 'dangerous activities' such as climbing, diving, horse riding, even trekking, if you plan to do any.

There are many insurance companies and policies to choose from, so it's best to shop around. Reputable student travel organizations often offer good value policies. Note that some companies will not cover those over 65 and you may need specialist services.

Language
English is the official language, but the language spoken by Jamaicans is Jamaican Creole, or Patois (Patwa, or Patwah). This is a language that developed in the 17th century as a means of communication between slaves from West and Central Africa and their European overseers, predominantly English, but with influences from Scottish, Irish, Spanish and Portuguese (see www.jumieka.com).

Money
US$1 = J$102.2; UK£1 = 163.7; €1 = J$138.2 (Sep 2013).

Currency
The Jamaican dollar (J$) is the local currency. It is divided into 100 cents. Banknotes in circulation are for J$50, 100, 500, 1000 and 5000. Coins in circulation are 1, 10 and 25 cents and J$1, 5, 10 and 20. The Bank of Jamaica (www.boj.org.jm) has details. The US dollar is widely accepted.

Plastic/currency cards/banks
The Jamaican dollar floats on the foreign exchange market. The only legal exchange transactions are those carried out in commercial banks, in official exchange bureaux called *cambios*, in major hotels and at the international airports. Retain your receipt so you can convert Jamaican dollars at the end of your stay. ATMs are available for international credit and debit cards, which can also be used to purchase goods and services. If using credit cards the transaction will be converted into US$ before you sign; be sure to verify the exact rate being used, often a 5-10% adjustment can be instantly obtained. If you don't want to carry lots of cash, prepaid currency cards allow you to preload money from your bank account, fixed at the day's exchange rate. They look like a credit or debit card and are issued by specialist money changing companies, such as **Travelex** and **Caxton FX**. You can top up and check your balance by phone, online and sometimes by text.

Cost of living/travelling
The cost of living in Jamaica is relatively high, much the same as in the UK or the US. For the best value, shop for locally made or produced items and beware mark-ups in shops catering specifically for the tourist trade. As a very rough guide, if your accommodation costs have already been paid for, allow US$50 a day for food and transport, assuming that you are taking no meals in your hotel. This does not include the price of tours or activities.

Opening hours
Banks: Mon-Fri varying between 0830 and 0900 to 1430 and 1530; banks usualy open later on Fri. **Offices**: Mon-Thu 0830-1700, till 1600 on Fri. **Shops**: Mon-Fri 0830-1630 or 1700, Sat 0800-1600, but in resort areas and in high season shops may keep much longer hours.

Post
There are post offices in all main towns. The central sorting office on South Camp Rd, Downtown Kingston, T922 9430, www.jamaicapost.gov.jm, has a good philatelic bureau.

Public holidays
1 Jan New Year's Day
Ash Wednesday
Good Friday
Easter Monday
23 May Labour Day
1 Aug Emancipation Day
6 Aug Independence Day
21 Oct National Heroes Day
25 Dec Christmas Day
26 Dec Boxing Day

Safety

The vast majority of Jamaicans welcome tourists and want to be helpful but the actions of the minority can leave you with the impression that tourists are not wanted. There are frequent military patrols to reinforce security in tourist areas. Downtown Montego Bay is patrolled by police on bikes and community involvement also helps to reduce harassment of tourists. Still, exercise caution when shopping and especially at nights.

The per capita crime rate is lower than in most North American cities, but there is a lot of violent crime. This is particularly concentrated in sections of downtown Kingston (90% of violent crime takes place in four Kingston police districts). While most incidents are community and turf related, crime can be encountered anywhere. Do not walk about in downtown Kingston after dark. There are large areas of west Kingston where you should not go off the main roads even by day. The motive is robbery so take sensible precautions. Beware of pickpockets and be firm but polite with touts. Do not wear jewellery. Do not go into the downtown areas of any towns at night. Avoid arriving in a town at night. Take a taxi from bus stations to your hotel. Travellers have reported incidents where Jamaicans have become aggressive over traffic accidents, however minor. Take the obvious precautions and you should have no problem.

Tax

Arrival and departure taxes Jamaica charges arriving air passengers 2 taxes of US$20 each (one called a Tourism Enhancement Fee and the other an Arrival Tax) and a departure tax of J$1800 (about US$18, payable in US dollars and other currencies), all of which are usually included in airline tickets. Cruise ship passengers are also charged a US$20 arrival tax. You may find that your ticket does not include some or all of these taxes. Check with your airline or all-inclusive package provider. **VAT** is called Gross Consumption Tax (GCT); for tourism businesses it is 10%, for other sectors 16.5%. There is also a **Guest Room Accommodation Tax**: US$1 for establishments with 1 to 50 rooms, US$2 for 51 to 100 rooms and US$4 over 101 rooms.

Telephone

Country code +876.

Landline and mobile services are provided by **LIME** (www.time4lime.com/jm), while **Digicel** (www.digiceljamaica.com) also provide mobile services. Before you leave home check with your mobile or smart phone provider whether your phone will work in Jamaica. With the right phone most apps etc should be accessible. Internet phone services are also available, but note that resorts often charge for Wi-Fi. It is also possible to buy or rent a mobile phone, or buy a local SIM card to put in your own phone (it must be unlocked).

Time

Eastern Standard Time, 5 hrs behind GMT and 1 hr behind the Eastern Caribbean.

Tipping

Hotel staff, waiters at restaurants, barmen, taxi drivers, cloakroom attendants and hairdressers get 10-15% of the bill. When service is included, personal tips are often still expected. In some areas you may be expected to tip when asking for information.

Tourist information

The **Jamaica Tourist Board** has offices at 64 Knutsford Blvd, Kingston 5, T929 9200, and 18 Queen's Drive, Montego Bay, T952 4425. Its website is www.visitjamaica.com, which has lots of information, including a list of offices overseas.

Useful websites

Jamaica Information Service, www.jis. gov.jm, official government news site. **Jamaica-No-Problem**, www.jamaica-no-problem.com, for news, tourist information, background information, details of community tourism, and more.

My Island Jamaica, www.my-island-jamaica.com, another news and information site, with a personal slant.
The Gleaner, www.jamaica-gleaner.com, daily newspaper
Jamaica Observer, www.jamaica observer.com, daily newspaper

Vaccinations

No vaccinations are required unless you have visited regions where yellow fever exists within 6 weeks of going to Jamaica, in which case you must provide a yellow fever vaccination certificate. Confirm that your primary courses and boosters are up to date. It is advisable to vaccinate against polio, tetanus, typhoid, hepatitis A and, for more remote areas, rabies.

Visas

Every visitor to Jamaica must have a passport valid for 6 months beyond the expected departure date and an onward ticket. Check online or at a Jamaican consulate to find out whether you need a visa. For limited stays a visa is not required for citizens of most Commonwealth countries (except British Virgin Islands, Nigeria, Pakistan and Sri Lanka) and some other countries (including EC, Scandinavia and Switzerland, Turkey and Germany).

Canadian and US citizens do not need passports or visas for a stay of up to 6 months, if they reside in their own countries and have proof of citizenship with photo ID (ie a birth certificate or certificate of citizenship), although Americans now need a passport to return to the USA. Citizens of all other countries must have a **visa**, **passport** and **onward ticket**. Immigration may insist on an onward address, before issuing an entry stamp. Hotel rooms can be booked at the airport tourist office. For visa extensions, apply to **Ministry of National Security, Immigration, Citizenship and Passport Services Department**, 25 Constant Spring Rd, Kingston 10, T906 1304. No vaccinations required unless you have visited Asia, Africa, Central or South America, Dominican Republic, Haiti, Trinidad or Tobago within 6 weeks of going to Jamaica.

Visas may be applied for at Jamaican embassies, consulates or high commissions and information can be found on sites such as www.jhcuk.org (Jamaican High Commission in the UK), www.congen jamaica-ny.org (Consulate General of Jamaica in New York) and www.visit jamaica.com. For visa extensions, apply to **Passport, Immigration and Citizenship Agency** of the Ministry of National Security, 25 Constant Spring Rd, Kingston 10, T754 4742, www.pica.gov.jm.

Contents

Footprint features

Jamaica

Kingston

Jamaica's capital since 1872 and the island's commercial centre, Kingston has the seventh best natural harbour in the world and its port is always busy. The city's population is about a third of the island's estimated total of 2.9 million people, squeezed into the flat lands between the sea and the mountains and spilling out to the sides, up into the Hellshire Hills, in an urban sprawl. The wealthy live up in the foothills of the Blue Mountains, their spacious houses benefiting from fresher air and breezes, while the poor live on the hot and dusty plains. Many are migrants from the countryside and continue to live a semi-rural life surrounded by their goats and chickens. Blocks of dwellings are known as 'yards' and it is here that political rivalries and gang warfare are fomented, leading to violence and crime. In the middle, the commercial and cultural centre is the hub of activity, a fast-paced city with theatres, museums, galleries and a wealth of restaurants, bars and clubs for entertainment. Kingstonians live life to the full, throwing themselves into festivals, Carnival and other exuberant activities. Music is everywhere, art fills the streets and sport is an obsession to be discussed animatedly and endlessly. Although it is not a city to walk around in the dark, by day it is as safe as any other and its streets are full of life, the pavements often crowded with higglers selling their wares on the ground in what is familiarly known as 'ben dung plaza' because you have to bend down (ben dung) to inspect the merchandise.

Arriving in Kingston

Getting there

The international airport for Kingston is the **Norman Manley** (restaurant, shops), 17 km away, up to 30 minutes' drive, on the peninsula opposite Kingston across the bay. There is also an airstrip for domestic flights at Tinson Pen Aerodrome, Marcus Garvey Drive, Kingston 11, 3 km from the centre. If you have flown in to Montego Bay on the north coast you can get to Kingston by aircharter flight or overland by frequent bus or car hire.

Getting around

Bus travel in Kingston costs US$1 for adults on the state-owned JUTC buses, while students in uniform, children, the disabled and pensioners pay half price, unless they have a Smart Card, in which case fares are US$0.20. Travelling by bus is safe and convenient and monitored by the **Transport Authority** ⓘ *T929 4642*. **Crossroads**, **Pechon Street** and **Half Way Tree** are the main bus stops. Addresses in the Parish of St Andrew have a numbered zone, eg Kingston 10, while those in the Parish of Kingston have no zone number and the address is just Kingston.

Tourist information

Jamaica Tourist Board ⓘ *Pan Caribbean Merchant Bank Building, 64 Knutsford Blvd, Kingston 5, T929 9200*. The Jamaica National Heritage Trust is a good source of heritage information, www.jnht.com.

Places in Kingston

Following the earthquake of 1907 much of the lower part of the city (Downtown) was rebuilt, replacing red bricks with concrete. The old racecourses have been redeveloped: the Kingston Race Track was converted to the National Heroes Park after independence in 1962 and the Knutsford Track was redeveloped in the 1960s as the New Kingston commercial district, which contains most of the big hotels and many banks and financial institutions. Kingston and the adjoining parish of St Andrew (Corporate Area) are busy traffic-clogged urban areas. The Corporate Area is dominated by commerce and central government, but Kingston is the cultural and intellectual hub of the island, offering a diversity of attractions and activities unmatched by any other parish. A city tour could extend as far as Devon House and the nearby Blue Mountains and beaches at Hellshire, Lime Cay and other cays off Port Royal, followed by several nightclubs. Reggae lovers should visit the Bob Marley Museum and the Tuff Gong recording studios, but music can be heard anywhere with frequent blasts from buses, bars and cars. There are several art galleries, institutes and museums worth paying a visit.

Downtown → *For listings, see pages 37-43.*

National Heroes Park

National Heroes Park is a good introduction to Jamaica's political and social development over the last couple of centuries, as it honours all those Jamaicans who have had a meaningful hand in shaping the way the country is today. Covering 74 acres, it was once the Kingston Race Course (1816-1953) until the track was moved to Knutsford Park, and was then called the George VI Memorial Park until independence from Great Britain in 1962.

Subsequently redesigned and renamed, three of Jamaica's National Heroes are buried here: Marcus Garvey, Sir Alexander Bustamante and Norman Washington Manley, while there are sculptures commemorating the lives of Bustamante, Manley, Bogle, Gordon, Sharpe, Garvey and Nanny of the Maroons. Notable Jamaicans such as past Prime Ministers, Michael Manley

① Kingston orientation

To Port Maria, Port Antonio & N Coast

CONSTANT SPRING

Constant Spring Golf Course

Red Hills

CONSTANT SPRING GARDENS

ALLERDYCE GARDENS

BARBICAN HEIGHTS

HUGHENDEN

Barbican Rd

BARBICAN

Hope Botanical Gardens

Taco Bell

Dunrobin Av

Washington Blvd

Jamaica House

King's House

Old Hope Rd

WASHINGTON GARDENS

Molynes Rd

WALTHAM FARM PARK

MONA HEIGHTS

FOUR MILE

HALF WAY TREE

NEW KINGSTON

Bob Marley Statue

Mona Reservoir

WHITFIELD

Retirement Rd

CROSS ROADS

National Stadium

Long Mountain

Hunts Bay

TRENCH TOWN

Calvary Cemetery

ALLMAN TOWN

TINSON PEN

Trench Town Culture Yard

National Heroes Park

FRANKLIN TOWN

Newport West

May Pen Cemetery

JONES TOWN

Sabina Park

Wembley Oval

Marcus Garvey Drive

Gordon House

Melbourne Park

Windward Rd

Newport East

Queen St

Harbour St

Sir William Grant Park

No 1 Pier

To Spanish Town, Montego Bay, North & West

To Papine & the Blue Mountains

To Norman Manley Airport & SE Coast

To Portmore

Kingston Harbour

Gallows Point

Refuge Cay

Royal Jamaica Yacht Club

Palisades Park

N Manley Highway

Port Royal Harbour

PORT ROYAL

The Palisades

Norman Manley Airport

Fort Charles

1 km
1 miles

N

Where to stay ▣
Christar Villas **1**
Gardens **2**
Medallion Hall **3**

Restaurants ❶
Tamarind Indian
Cuisine **1**
Medusa's **2**

➡ **Kingston maps**
1 Kingston orientation, page 26
2 Downtown Kingston, page 29
3 New Kingston, page 32

and Sir Donald Sangster are buried in the cemetery to the north, reserved for those who have contributed to the political, social and educational development of the country. Here you will find the Jamaica War Memorial, with the largest cenotaph on the island, protected by the Jamaica Defence Force. The ceremonial changing of the guard takes place on the first Sunday of the month at 0900 to the musical accompaniment of a military band, although you can catch the regular changing of the guard 10 minutes to the hour every day from 0800-1700 when the soldiers go through their drills.

Jamaica National Heritage Trust

The Jamaica National Heritage Trust can be found in one of the older buildings of note in the Downtown area: **Headquarters House** ① *8179 Duke St, T922 1287, www.jnht.com*, which dates from the mid-18th century. Formerly called Hibbert House, it was one of several large mansions built at that time by wealthy merchants. Thomas Hibbert, who built the house in the English Georgian style with the aim of owning the most beautiful home in the country, was a merchant but also, from 1756, the Speaker of the House of Assembly. For a time their meetings were held there. In 1814, it became the headquarters and residence of the British Royal Army General stationed in Kingston. After a subsequent spell as the offices of the Colonial Secretary, it became the permanent seat of the Jamaica Legislature from 1872-1960. It was then replaced by **Gordon House**, the modern building next door, as the seat of Jamaica's parliament. George William Gordon, after whom the building is named, was a member of the House of Assembly in the mid-19th century. He is one of Jamaica's National Heroes for speaking out against the treatment of blacks by the white rulers. He was accused of colluding with Paul Bogle, the leader of the 1865 rebellion, and was later sentenced to death.

Sha'are Shalom Synagogue

① *Duke St on the corner with Charles St, T927 7948.*

Also in this area is this synagogue, the last one left on Jamaica, and home to the United Congregation of Israelites. Jews have a long history in Jamaica and the first synagogue was built in Port Royal in 1646, although it did not survive the earthquake of 1692. There used to be synagogues all over the island as Jewish immigration rose, but congregations have since dwindled. This white building dates from 1912.

Parade and around

Parade (Sir William Grant Park, named in honour of the 1938 labour leader who was an associate of Sir Alexander Bustamante) is at the heart of the city centre; it is an open oasis amid the densely packed surroundings. The park is at the junction of the main east-west route through the Downtown area (Windward Road/East Queen Street-West Queen Street/Spanish Town Road) and King Street/Orange Street, which runs north to Cross Roads, and is a hub for public transport. The name Parade derives from the British soldiers' parades here during colonial rule and the gardens were laid out in 1870 after they moved to Up Park Camp. There are several monuments, chief of which is of Queen Victoria, after whom the park was originally named until independence. To the north is the statue of National Hero Norman Manley, facing Upper King Street, and to the south the statue of Sir Alexander Bustamante. He is depicted baring his chest, daring the police to shoot him, as he did in political rallies in the 1930s. Also overlooking the Parade is Edna Manley's famous bronze statue *Negro Aroused*, a larger version of the wooden original inside the National Gallery, created as a monument to those involved in the 1938 labour riots. On the north

Dreadlocks to reggae

Followers of the Rastafarian cult are non-violent, do not eat pork and believe in the divinity of the late Emperor of Ethiopia, Haile Selassie (Ras Tafari). Haile Selassie's call for the end of the superiority of one race over another has been incorporated into a faith which holds that God, Jah, will lead the blacks out of oppression (Babylon) back to Ethiopia (Zion, the Promised Land). The Rastas regard the ideologist Marcus Garvey (born 1887, St Ann's Bay) as a prophet of the return to Africa (he is now a Jamaican national hero). In the early 20th century, Garvey founded the idea of black nationalism, with Africa as the home for blacks, whether they are living on the continent or not.

The music most strongly associated with Rastafarianism is reggae. According to OR Dathorne, "it is evident that the sound and words of Jamaican reggae have altered the life of the English-speaking Caribbean. The extent of this alteration is still unknown, but this new sound has touched, more than any other single art medium, the consciousness of the people of this region" (*Dark Ancestor*, page 229, Louisiana State University Press, 1981). The sound is a mixture of African percussion and up-to-the-minute electronics; the lyrics are a blend of praise of Jah, political comment and criticism and the mundane. The late Bob Marley, the late Peter Tosh, Dennis Brown and Jimmy Cliff are among Jamaica's most famous reggae artists. Over the last few years, traditional reggae has been supplanted by Dancehall Reggae, which has a much heavier beat, with new artists such as Grammy winners Shabba Ranks and Junior Gong, son of Bob Marley. Also closely related to reggae is dub poetry, a chanted verse form that combines the musical tradition, folk traditions and popular speech. Its first practitioner was Louise Bennett, in the 1970s, who has been followed by poets such as Linton Kwesi Johnson, Michael Smith, Oku Onora and Mutabaruka. Many of these poets work in the UK, but their links with Jamaica are strong. The dancehall culture has spawned its own genre of poets, as some young and upcoming artists give vent to their feelings on the growing social divide. One such group is the popular Twins Of Twins, Paul and Patrick Gaynor, song writers and poets whose talented writings bring the painful experience of the ghetto to their audiences through humorous but deeply reflective social commentary.

Two novels which give a fascinating insight into Rasta culture (and, in the latter, Revival and other social events) are *Brother Man*, by Roger Mais, and *The Children of Sysiphus*, by H Orlando Patterson. These writers have also published other books that are worth investigating, as are the works of Olive Senior (eg *Summer Lightning*), and the poets Mervyn Morris, the late Andrew Salkey and Dennis Scott (who is also involved in the theatre).

side of the square is the **Ward Theatre**. There has been a theatre here since 1777 although this building dates from 1912 and was a gift to the city from Colonel Ward, who made his money from selling rum and other alcohol through the family firm of J Wray & Nephew, of which he was the nephew. This is the place to come for the annual pantomime, a tradition for decades which starts on 26 December and runs until March. There is also the **Kingston Parish Church** south of Parade, also known as the Church of St Thomas the Apostle. Although the church was rebuilt in 1909, the cemetery contains graves dating

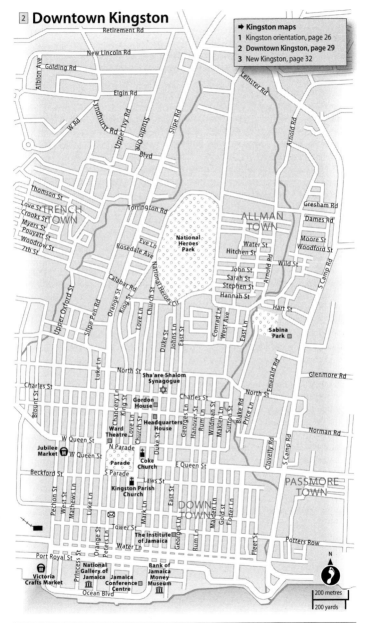

➜ **Kingston maps**
1 Kingston orientation, page 26
2 Downtown Kingston, page 29
3 New Kingston, page 32

Retirement Rd
New Lincoln Rd
Albion Ave
Golding Rd
Elgin Rd
Lyndhurst Rd
W Rd
Upper Ivy Rd
Studio One Blvd
Slipe Rd
Leinster Rd
Arnold Rd
Thomson St
TRENCH TOWN
Love St
Crooks St
Myers St
Pouyatt St
Woodrow St
7th St
Torrington Rd
Eve Ln
Rosedale Ave
Calabar Rd
Gresham Rd
Dames Rd
Moore St
Woodford St
ALLMAN TOWN
National Heroes Park
Water St
Hitchen St
John St
Sarah St
Stephen St
Hannah St
Upper Oxford St
Slipe Pen Rd
Orange St
King St
Love Ln
Church St
National Heroes Cir
Duke St
Johns Ln
East St
Conrad St
West Ave
Hart St
East Ln
Sabina Park
Luke Ln
North St
Emerald Rd
Glenmore Rd
Charles St
Bloutt St
Chancery Ln
King St
Love Ln
Church St
Sha'are Shalom Synagogue
Gordon House
Charles St
Georges St
Hanover St
Wildman St
Makien St
Sutton St
Blake Rd
Price Ln
North St
Clovelly Rd
Norman Rd
S Camp Rd
Ward Theatre
Headquarters House
Duke St
Jubilee Market
W Queen St
W Queen St
N Parade
Coke Church
E Queen St
PASSMORE TOWN
Beckford St
Parade
S Parade
Pechon St
West St
Mathews Ln
Luke Ln
Kingston Parish Church
Laws St
Mark Ln
East St
Maiden Ln
Gold St
Foster Ln
DOWN TOWN
Tower St
The Institute of Jamaica
Georges St
Rum Ln
Fleet St
Potters Row
Port Royal St
Orange St
Peters St
Water Ln
Victoria Crafts Market
National Gallery of Jamaica
Princess St
Jamaica Conference Centre
Bank of Jamaica Money Museum
Ocean Blvd

N

200 metres
200 yards

back to 1699, including that of Admiral Benbow, while inside there are plaques to many worthy citizens. In 1789 a Wesleyan missionary, the Rev Dr Coke, arrived in Jamaica and in 1790 opened a chapel on the eastern side of the park. The authorities soon had it closed, because of the missionaries' work with slaves, but the present 19th century red brick **Coke Church** at the corner with East Queen Street stands on the site of that Methodist chapel.

The waterfront
On the waterfront there are some notable modern buildings including the **Bank of Jamaica**, which houses the **Money Museum** ① *Nethersole Pl, T922 0750, Mon-Fri 1000-1600, free*, with a fine selection of old tokens, notes and coins used during the colonial era, including pieces of eight and Taíno gold; the **Jamaica Conference Centre** and the **National Gallery of Jamaica** ① *12 Ocean Blvd, Block C, entrance on Orange St, T922 1561, Tue-Thu 1000-1630, Fri 1000-1600, Sat 1000-1500, US$4*. Well worth seeing, the gallery has a wide selection of Jamaican art, both paintings and sculptures and is an excellent introduction to the talent produced by Jamaica over the last century or so. This is the place to come to see the work of Edna Manley (1900-1987), the 20th century's foremost Jamaican artist and hugely influential, being the wife of former Prime Minister, Norman Manley, and the mother of former Prime Minister, Michael Manley. You can also see works by Carl Abrahams, Cecil Baugh, Mallica 'Kapo' Reynolds, David Boxer, Dawn Scott and John Dunkley, some of whose work is on permanent display. The gallery hosts temporary exhibitions on a variety of themes and encourages young Jamaican artists, supporting up and coming talent. In 2013, the **Victoria Crafts Market** on the waterfront to the west received a face lift to improve conditions for both vendors and tourists. Asbestos was removed, roof repairs were carried out, the building was repainted and new seating and eating areas were constructed. Having suffered from a poor reputation for safety, and a steady decline in its attraction, it is to be hoped that the beautification will result in more customers visiting and buying the basketwork, clothing and carvings so representative of Jamaican artistic skills.

The Institute of Jamaica and the National Library
The Institute of Jamaica was established in 1879, in an elegant red brick building, by Sir Anthony Musgrave, then Governor of Jamaica ① *10-16 East St, T922 0620, Mon-Thu 0830-1799, Fri 0830-1600*. It is Jamaica's oldest museum, set up for 'the Encouragement of Literature, Science and Art in Jamaica' and has under its control the National Museum Jamaica, the National Gallery of Jamaica, the Natural History Museum of Jamaica, the Jamaica Music Museum, the African Caribbean Institute of Jamaica/Jamaica Memory Bank, the Junior Centres and Liberty Hall: Legacy of Marcus Garvey. The Natural History Museum has an interactive display of Jamaica's fauna and flora, which is particularly child-friendly. There is also a herbarium and a Zoology department with an extensive collection of spiders and insects. The Science Library has scientific publications and journals going back to the 18th century. Adjoining the Institute is **The National Library**, housing books, documents and newspapers going back to the 18th century, one of the most important collections in the English-speaking Caribbean. A wide range of temporary exhibitions take place at any time, check the website for what's on.

On the west side of Parade is the **Jubilee Market**, an enormous conglomeration of stalls selling everything from fruit and veg, meat and fish, herbs and spices (some not so legal), to household items, plastic goods and CDs. Part of the market is covered, but stalls spill out into the streets around and the whole area is raucous, untidy and very Jamaican. Do not take valuables into this area and watch out for pickpockets. Some people don't mind being photographed, but others take offence and can get abusive, so it is best to ask permission.

West of downtown

West of downtown Kingston, near the May Pen Cemetery, is the **Trench Town Culture Yard**, a project started by the **Trench Town Development Association (TTDA)** ① *6-10 Lower First St, Trench Town, Kingston 12, T376 0891, see Facebook*, a community-based NGO, to boost the inner-city community of Trench Town, concentrating on the reggae heritage of Bob Marley and other great musicians who came from the area. The Trench Town Culture Yard, now a National Heritage Site, is the 'government yard' where Bob Marley and the Wailers lived and composed many of their best known songs in the 1970s. These yards were very basic, with 10-20 rooms built around a common cooking and washing area. Bob Marley's yard has 16 rooms; you can see his bedroom and bed, his first guitar and the shell of his VW camper van. There are also photographs and documents showing the history of Trench Town. There isn't much to see, but a guide will give you a detailed picture of the history and community. Trench Town was developed in the 1940s as a 200-acre model community, but the growth of political violence and gang warfare dragged the area into poverty. Nevertheless, it spawned talent, notably Bob Marley, Peter Tosh, Bunny Wailer, the Abyssinians and the Heptones.

New Kingston → *For listings, see pages 37-43.*

At Cross Roads, north of National Heroes Park, the main route forks, left to Half Way Tree, the capital of St Andrew, and straight on up Old Hope Road to Liguanea. These two roads encompass New Kingston. Cross Roads is a busy junction, marking the move from Downtown to Up Town. The clock tower here was put up in memory of the Jamaican servicemen who were killed in the Second World War. The Carib Theatre was the city's main concert hall in the early 20th century and then a cinema but after it burned down in 1996 it was rebuilt as a multi-screen cinema.

Emancipation Park

Head up Half Way Tree Road and at the junction with Oxford Road you come to Emancipation Park. Close to several of the hotels in New Kingston, it is well-used as an open space by joggers early morning and evening, the lunchtime office crowd and for concerts at night. It is also the site of a large bronze statue by Laura Facey Cooper, called *Redemption Song*. Depicting a naked man and a naked woman emerging from the water gazing up to the sky, the artist faced criticism from the public when they were unveiled in 2003. Symbolizing the suffering of slavery being washed away by the water and the pair standing in unity and strength, they nevertheless shocked many for their nakedness, in particular the rather well-endowed man.

Half Way Tree and around

The Parish Church at St Andrew at Half Way Tree dates from 1700, although it has undergone many renovations over the centuries. Half Way Tree was a half-way stage on the road between Spanish Town, the then capital, and the hills. Half Way Tree is conspicuously marked by an old clock tower and a public park (recently renamed Nelson Mandela Park). It is a busy junction which takes some negotiating in a car.

The two parishes of Kingston and St Andrew together form the **Corporate Area** (Kingston being that section of the Corporate Area south of the National Heroes Park) and St Andrew being to the north. Most of the new shops and offices are in the Parish of St Andrew, although visitors and even locals are often not aware of where one parish ends and the next begins. Crossroads and Half Way Tree (St Andrew) are referred to as midtown areas. Many shopping plazas are further north again along the **Constant Spring Road** and east along **Old Hope Road** to Liguanea.

3 New Kingston

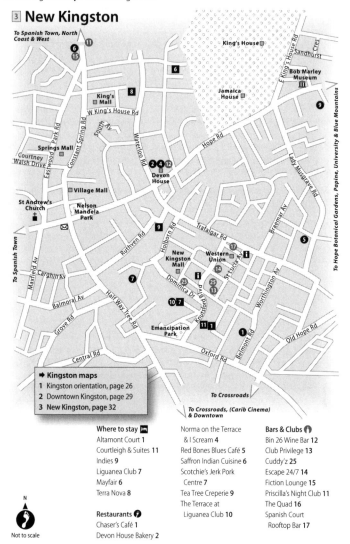

➔ **Kingston maps**
1 Kingston orientation, page 26
2 Downtown Kingston, page 29
3 New Kingston, page 32

Where to stay 🛏
Altamont Court 1
Courtleigh & Suites 11
Indies 9
Liguanea Club 7
Mayfair 6
Terra Nova 8

Restaurants 🍴
Chaser's Café 1
Devon House Bakery 2

Norma on the Terrace
 & I Scream 4
Red Bones Blues Café 5
Saffron Indian Cuisine 6
Scotchie's Jerk Pork
 Centre 7
Tea Tree Creperie 9
The Terrace at
 Liguanea Club 10

Bars & Clubs 🍸
Bin 26 Wine Bar 12
Club Privilege 13
Cuddy'z 25
Escape 24/7 14
Fiction Lounge 15
Priscilla's Night Club 11
The Quad 16
Spanish Court
 Rooftop Bar 17

N

Not to scale

Devon House
ⓘ *Waterloo and Hope roads.*

Just a few minutes' drive to the east of Half Way Tree along Hope Road is Devon House, built like a 'great house' in the 1880s by Jamaica's first negro millionaire, George Stiebel, who made his money in South America and caused quite a stir in Jamaica. It is said that Lady Musgrave's Road was built because the Governor's wife did not like driving in her carriage to church past Devon House, which was grander than hers. It has been under renovation and closed to the public for several years, but you can still visit the gardens. There are craft shops and restaurants in the grounds and this is a popular green space for residents and visitors alike, with students lying on the grass studying and office workers taking a break. Most come for the food – there are delicious patties and pastries – and especially the ice cream, which is superb, with some great local flavours. If you want a full meal, **Norma's on the Terrace** is one of the top restaurants on the island.

Not far away is **King's House** ⓘ *corner of Hope Rd and East King's House Rd*, the official residence of the Governor-General, set in grounds of 200 acres (80 ha) and, nearby is **Jamaica House** ⓘ *Hope Rd*, the office of the Prime Minister.

Bob Marley Museum
ⓘ *56 Hope Rd, T978 2991/927 9152, www.bobmarley-foundation.com/museum.html, Mon-Sat, 1st tour 0930, last tour -1600, non-resident adults US$20, 4-12s US$10, including obligatory 1-hr guided tour and 20-min audio visual presentation, no photos inside the house.*

About 10 blocks east of Devon House is the house where Marley used to live, which traces his story back to the time of his childhood and family, with paintings, newspaper cuttings, posters and other memorabilia. He died tragically of brain cancer in 1981 at the age of 36, having survived a controversial assassination attempt (the bullet-holes in the walls have been left as a reminder). There is a gift shop selling Jamaican and African artefacts. Marijuana plants grow profusely throughout the grounds and ganja is smoked openly by staff.

Hope Royal Botanical Gardens
ⓘ *See Facebook, 0600-1800, free, parking US$2.*

Further east, along Old Hope Road, are the Hope Royal Botanical Gardens. The land was first acquired by Major Richard Hope in 1671 and 200 years later the Governor of Jamaica, Sir John Peter Grant, bought 81 ha and created the gardens. In 1961 a **zoo** ⓘ *T927 1085, daily 0600-1800, US$15, 3-11s US$10*, was opened alongside the gardens, now a showcase for the different habitats of Jamaica and its indigenous animals. Both the zoo and the gardens have lost much of their former glory because of a lack of government financial support, but the gardens are still a pleasant spot for a picnic and families come here at weekends to relax. The Royal Botanic Gardens and Plant Nursery are managed and operated by the non-government Nature Preservation Foundation.

University of the West Indies and the National Stadium
Beyond Hope Gardens is Papine and the University of the West Indies, its residences and the University Hospital of the West Indies. The Mona Campus is on an old sugar estate, and you can still see the remains of the aqueduct and old sugar mill. An old sugar warehouse from Trelawny has been brought here and converted to a chapel. If you go in through the hospital gate and drive out of Queen's gate (collect parking permit on entering and give it up at exit), you come out on Mona Road, passing under an aqueduct which is still in use, bringing water from Hope River to Mona reservoir. Heading south again down Old Hope

Cool Runnings

Jamaica is not known for its winter sports: there is no snow on the Blue Mountain range and its lakes never freeze over. However, Jamaicans can run and they are fiercely competitive in sports, so a few of them decided to enter a bobsled team in the 1988 Winter Olympics. They had had very little practice when they arrived in Calgary and they had very little equipment, but they were given help and advice from other teams and massive support from the crowd, who saw them as the ultimate underdogs to cheer for. That first team of Devon Harris, Dudley Stokes, Michael White and Nelson Stokes did not officially finish as they crashed on one of their runs, but they were clearly improving. On the basis that practice makes perfect, they entered again in 1992, where they finished, but well outside any rankings, and in 1994 in Lillehammer, where they stunned everyone by finishing in 14th place, ahead of the USA.

The 1998 effort inspired a major movie, *Cool Runnings*, and brought the team international fame beyond bobsled aficionados. In the film, after the crash, the four men pick themselves up and walk across the finish line carrying their sled. That didn't happen in real life, but they did pick themselves up and walk down the run, smiling and shaking hands with the crowd as they went. See www.youtube.com/watch?v=nm4DjRcmoPY.

That wasn't the end of winter sports for Jamaica. In 2005 Danny Melville, owner of Chukka Caribbean Adventures, came across a dryland cart for training dog teams when he was shopping for dune buggies. Intrigued, he had one made and sent Chukka Cove manager, Devon Anderson, to Scotland to train in dryland racing. They acquired nine dogs from a Jamaican dog rescue home, built kennels and started to train them to pull the cart. In 2006 Anderson travelled to Scotland again and to Minnesota to compete in dryland races. Jamaican dogs are not allowed back into the country once they have left, so he had to hire teams of dogs, leaving the dogs he trained with at home. With very respectable results, the media started to take an interest and a documentary, *Sun Dogs*, was made. In 2007 Damian Robb and Newton Marshall joined the team, now sponsored by Jimmy Buffett, training with experts abroad and practising with the rescue dogs at home. Then, in 2008, they started competing on snow, Robb concentrating on sprint racing, coming seventh in his first race, and Marshall building up his strength for long-distance racing when Anderson dropped out. Marshall came seventh in his first race too, from Dawson City, Yukon, to Eagle, Alaska, and back. He was also given the Sportsmanship award, the Race Marshall calling him 'the coolest guy out there'. Marshall continued to clock up the miles, becoming the first Caribbean and the first black musher to complete the 1100-mile Iditarod race from Willow to Nome, Alaska, finishing 47th out of 71 mushers in a time of 12 days, four hours, 27 minutes, 28 seconds. In the same year, Robb won a sprint race and came second and third a couple of times.

The Jamaican team continued to compete abroad, while their Jamaican dogs stayed home, taking tourists on adventure tours in their dryland carts. However, in 2013 the team and the dogs retired. The dogs found new adoptive homes and Jimmy Buffett, the principal team sponsor for eight years, was helping the team make a movie – of course.

Road, fork left down Mountain View Avenue and then turn right along Stadium Boulevard by the **National Stadium**, where major sporting events are held. At the entrance to the Stadium is a statue by Alvin Marriott symbolizing Jamaican athletic prowess, while another of his statues is across the drive to the National Arena, beside the National Stadium, that of **Bob Marley**. The first statue commissioned after the singer's death, from Christopher Gonzalez, was so unpopular that is was removed to the National Gallery and this, more realistic likeness, was its replacement. In 1978, Bob Marley's great One Love Concert for Peace was held in the National Stadium, and when he died in 1981, his body lay in state here while 30,000 people filed past to pay their respects. His Rastafari funeral service was held in the National Arena.

Up Park Camp

Arthur Wint Drive heads southwest from here to Up Park Camp, just east of Cross Roads. Arthur Wint was a Jamaican athlete who won gold in the 400 m at the 1948 London Olympic Games and was a member of the 4 x 400-m relay team which won gold at the 1952 Helsinki Olympic Games. Up Park Camp, or 'Camp' as it is usually known, was built in 1784 for British regiments stationed in Jamaica and is now the Jamaica Defence Force Headquarters. The southern entrance is named Duppy Gate. Legend has it that the ghost of an officer of the West India Regiment used to call out the guard there for inspection. South Camp Road runs south from here all the way to the harbour, passing Sabina Park, Kingston's Test cricket ground since 1930. This attractive ground has played host to some fantastic matches and all the world's best cricketers have played here. Sir Garfield Sobers' 365 not out scored here stood as a Test record for over 36 years. George Headley, player, captain of the West Indies and coach during the colonial era, has a stand named after him and a statue at its entrance by Jamaican sculptor Basil Watson. Upgraded for the 2007 Cricket World Cup it has a capacity of 20,000,

Around Kingston → *For listings, see pages 37-43.*

Port Royal

ⓘ *Beyond the international airport, some 24 km by excellent road.*

Port Royal, the old naval base, lies across the harbour from Kingston. It was founded in 1650, captured by the English and turned into a strategic military and naval base. Merchant shipping developed under naval protection and the town soon became prosperous. It also attracted less reputable shipping and in 1660-1692 became a haven for pirates such as Henry Morgan, with gambling and drinking dens and brothels protected by the six forts and 145 guns. The 'wickedest city on earth', with a population of 8000, soon provoked what was thought to be divine retribution. On 7 June 1692 an earthquake hit east Jamaica, coursing along the Port Royal fault line and bringing with it massive tidal waves. The port, commercial area and harbour front were cut away and slid down the slope of the bay to rest on the sea bed, while much of the rest of the town was flooded for weeks. About 5000 people died (of drowning, injuries or subsequent disease) and the naval, merchant and fishing fleets were wrecked. The town was gradually rebuilt as a naval and military post but has had to withstand 16 hurricanes, nine earthquakes, three fires and a storm (which in 1951 left only four buildings undamaged).

Nelson served here as a post-captain from 1779 to 1780 and commanded **Fort Charles**, built in 1655 and first named Fort Cromwell, key battery in the island's fortifications, with 34 guns by 1667. A hundred years later it was recorded as having 104 guns and a garrison of 500 men. The former British naval headquarters now house the **Fort Charles Maritime Museum** ① *daily 0900-1645, US$5, children US$2*, with a scale model of the fort and ships. Part of the ramparts, known as **Nelson's Quarterdeck**, still stands. The **Giddy House** was the Royal Artillery store, built in 1888 but damaged by the 1907 earthquake, which caused it to tilt at an angle of 45°. The Victoria Albert battery complex was a boiler house and underground armoury with late 19th-century guns to protect the harbour and tunnels. The old naval hospital was built in 1819 of prefabricated cast-iron sections brought all the way from England, one of the earliest constructions of this type and built on a raft foundation. The old gaol can also be seen. This dates from the early 18th century and was used as a women's prison in the 19th century. **St Peter's Church** is of historic interest, though the restoration is unfortunate. The **National Museum of Historical Archaeology** ① *Mon-Sat 1000-1700, US$2*, is little more than one room and the Fort Charles remains are more informative and substantive.

Boats may be hired for picnics on the numerous nearby cays or at Port Henderson. **Lime Cay** (about the size of a football pitch) is the most popular, offering a white-sand beach and crystal clear water. A seafood restaurant and bar provides tasty fried fish and chicken meals. There is a full service marina at **Morgan's Harbour** with customs clearance, 24-hour security and fishing boats for hire.

Spanish Town

Spanish Town, the former capital, founded in 1534 and some 23 km west of Kingston (bus from Half Way Tree and from Orange Street), is historically the most interesting of Jamaica's towns. The first settlement was called Villa de la Vega, founded by the Spanish Governor, Francisco de Garay, who made it the capital of the colony. Later it was called Santiago de la Vega or San Jago de la Vega. The Taíno had been living in the area before the arrival of the Spanish. The British conquered the island in 1655 and referred to it as Spanish Town, but it was badly damaged during fighting and had to be rebuilt. Port Royal became the chief administrative town and unofficial capital for a while. By the time Port Royal was destroyed by the 1692 earthquake, Spanish Town had been rebuilt and it remained the capital until Kingston took over the mantle in 1872. The decline of Spanish Town started long before then, however, with no real commercial activity to sustain it and it could not compete with the natural advantages and thriving harbour of Kingston. The town has a fine Georgian main square, a very British architectural style transported to the tropics, from where the proclamation ending slavery in 1838 was read. Street names invoke past glories from both the Spanish and British eras. Red Church Street and White Church Street refer to the Spanish chapels of the red and white cross, while Monk Street refers to the monastery which once featured there. King Street runs in front of the King's House, the governor's residence; Nugent Street is named after a British colonial governor, George Nugent, as is Manchester Street, named after William Montagu, fifth Duke of Manchester.

The **Cathedral Church of St James**, the oldest in the anglophone West Indies, dates back to 1714 after a hurricane destroyed the previous building in 1712. It has thick, red brick walls and replaced the Spanish cathedral on the same site, adjoining the prison. A mixture of styles, it even has a tower, added in 1817, with a steeple, not commonly found in the Caribbean. It is also known as the St Catherine Parish Church and several colonial governors are buried here among other worthy dignitaries. The square houses the ruins of the **King's House**, built in 1762 (Governor's residence until 1872 when Kingston became the capital) and burnt down in 1925. The façade has been rebuilt and beside it is the **Jamaican People's Museum of Craft and Technology** ① *Mon-Thu, 0930-1630*,

Fri 0930-1530, US$2, children US$1. Created in 1961 as the Folk Museum, it got its present name in 1979 and contains lots of tools and artefacts used in daily life over the centuries. Also on the square are a colonnade and statue commemorating Rodney's victory at the Battle of the Saints, the **House of Assembly** (now local government offices) and the **Courthouse** (in ruins). Outside town, on the road to Kingston, is the **Iron Bridge** over the Rio Cobre River. It is no longer in use, having been closed in 1931 when Stubbs Bridge was built, but you can get a good view of it from Stubbs Bridge parallel to it over the river. Built in 1801 and designed by Thomas Wilson, it is the oldest bridge of its type in the Americas and is about 81 ft long and 15 ft wide.

Kingston listings

For hotel and restaurant price codes and other relevant information, see pages 12-14.

🛏 Where to stay

Kingston *p24, maps p26 and p32*
$$$$ Courtleigh Hotel and Suites,
85 Knutsford Blvd, Kingston 5, T929 9000, www.courtleigh.com. 126 1- and 2-bedroom suites, fine if you're on expenses, business centre and meeting facilities, internet access in rooms, multilingual staff, gym, pool, magnificent view of city, harbour and mountains, quietest rooms with best views on higher floors, **Alexander's Restaurant** and **Mingles Pub** on site.
$$$$ Spanish Court, 1 St Lucia Av, Kingston 5, T926 0000, www.spanish courthotel.com. A very popular hotel offering a good standard of accommodation and service. Rooms and suites in an attractive, Spanish-style building, conveniently located. Great breakfasts and other meals are good too with romantic poolside dining and live music.
$$$$ Strawberry Hill, Newcastle Rd, up in the hills of Irish Town overlooking Kingston Bay, T944 8400, www.islandoutpost.com. Now a 12-villa luxury retreat but formerly a coffee and fruit plantation house, sadly destroyed by Hurricane Gilbert in 1988. Elegant, traditionally furnished cottages, enchanting gardens, breathtaking views, especially from the infinity pool. Gourmet dinners, brunches, lunches and tea, also sophisticated entertainment. Recommended

weekend brunch of real Jamaican dishes such as jerk meats, ackee and salt fish, followed by Jamaican desserts and fresh fruits, washed down with a cocktail or fruit punch and then Blue Mountain coffee, US$40 for as much as you can eat, reservations recommended. Full service spa, conference, banquet and wedding facilities.
$$$$ Terra Nova, 17 Waterloo Rd, Kingston 10, T926 2211, www.terranovajamaica.com. Recently upgraded suites in a 1924 mansion, former family home and birthplace of Chris Blackwell, the record producer. Very elegant, antiques and custom-made furniture, popular with business travellers, conference facilities and business centre, pool, bar, café and restaurant with excellent cuisine on the terrace or in the **Regency Room**. Live entertainment by the pool bar.
$$$$-$$$ Altamont Court, 1-5 Altamont Terrace, Kingston 5, T929 4497, www. altamontcourt.com. Comfortable rooms and suites, fridge on request, pool, restaurant, full Jamaican breakfast, gym, facilities for the disabled, meeting rooms, multilingual staff.
$$$$-$$$ Christar Villas, 99A Hope Rd, Kingston 6, T978 3933, www.christarvillas hotel.com. 32, 1- or 2-bedroom suites and studios with kitchenettes, pool, spa, sports bar, restaurant, small gym, conference facilities and business centre, free airport shuttle 0800-1700. Some of the facilities are past their best but the staff try hard to please.
$$$ The Gardens, 23 Liguanea Av, Kingston 6, T927 8275, www.gardensjamaica.com. Town houses, with 2 rooms, private

bathrooms and shared living and dining room downstairs, rent a room or the whole house, pool, homely service, convenient location within walking distance of Sovereign Shopping Mall and the bus route, also close to the university.

$$$ Indies, 5 Holborn Rd, Kingston 10, T926 2952, www.indieshotel.com. 15 rooms, singles, doubles and triples, cheapest option for single travellers, price depends on fan or a/c, TV or cable TV, nothing fancy but comfortable, pleasant patio, garden, helpful owners, relaxed family atmosphere.

$$$ Liguanea Club, Knutsford Blvd, Kingston 5, T968 3483, www.theliguanea club.com. A sports club in the centre of the city with 38 simple guest rooms, good for business travellers who want a game of tennis or squash to unwind. Friendly service and good food, but events at weekends can bring very loud music.

$$$ Medallion Hall, 53 Hope Rd, Kingston 6, T927 3484, medallionhall hotel@yahoo.com. 22 elegant a/c rooms with Victorian-style furniture, wheelchair access, conference rooms, restaurant, central. Very friendly, helpful, excellent service, family-friendly.

$$$ Neita's Nest, Stony Hill, St Andrew, T469 3005, www.neitasnest.com. About 15 mins from New Kingston in the suburban area of Bridgemount, north of Manor Park, this 3-bedroomed B&B is charming, friendly and comfortable with glorious views of green, forested hills from the veranda. Good birdwatching.

$$$ Rafjam's Bed & Breakfast, 6-8 Springdale Cove, Hopewell, T426 3667, www.rafjam.net. Delightful small B&B in the mountains where the air is cooler and the pace of life is slower. Susan has built up this property into something special, comfortable, with good food and service. Lovely gardens and views in a remote part of the hills.

$$ Mount Edge Guest House & EITS Café, 17 Mile Post, Newcastle, T944 8151. Very rural, perched up on the mountainside

in the heart of the countryside yet only 30 mins by car from Kingston. Rustic rooms and cottages, some with shared bathroom, peaceful, a good way to get to know Jamaica. All veg grown locally. People come out from Kingston at weekends for lunch.

🍴 Restaurants

Kingston *p24, maps p26 and p32*
There are many places, plush and modest, to eat in **Downtown Kingston**, **New Kingston**, **Half Way Tree** and the **Liguanea** area. For the impecunious, meat patties can be bought for about US$1.20 each from **Tastee**, **Juici Patties** or **Mother's**, various locations but mostly in **Liguanea**, **Half Way Tree**, **New Kingston**, **Cross Roads** or **Manor Park**. Fillings are usually beef, chicken, cheese, soya, shrimp, lobster or vegetable. Every Jamaican has his/her own favourite brand and will probably tell you they aren't as good as they used to be. Also a wide range of lovely cakes and pastries. On Knutsford Blvd there are lots of vans selling a satisfying cheap lunch.

$$$ Chaser's Café, 5 Belmont Rd, Kingston 5, T908 0524, see Facebook. Bar and restaurant with lots of specials from a full Sun brunch at 0900 sharp with all the Jamaican favourites, to Karaoke Mon, Seafood Thu and their famous Wed crab night, when you can eat crab in a wide variety of styles. Also good after hours, when their rum and coconut water will get you up and dancing.

$$$ East Japanese, The Market Pl, 67 Constant Spring Rd, T960 3962, www.eat japaneserestaurantsja.webs.com. Open 1200-2230. Good Japanese food with sushi bar, dine in at tables, at the bar or takeaway.

$$$ EITS Café, 17 Mile Post, Newcastle, T944 8151, www.17milepost.com. Up a steep and winding road from Kingston into the mountains, but worth the effort for the view and the food. Good fresh food, using veg and herbs from the farm, delicious salads. Open for breakfast, lunch and a romantic dinner, also popular with Kingstonians for weekend brunch.

$$$ Medusa's, 96 Hope Rd, T978 3741. A good bar and restaurant particularly popular on Fri night, which is grill night. You can have chicken, pork, lobster, etc, but the star of the show is the 10-oz steak for US$15, perfectly cooked just how you like it with any number of sides, such as corn, baked or mashed potatoes, mushrooms, vegetables, salad. Go early or they may run out.

$$$ Norma's on the Terrace, Devon House (see page 33), 26 Hope Rd, Kingston 10, entrance on Waterloo Rd, T968 5488. One of the best restaurants in the city, outdoor seating under cover with fans to keep you cool. Lunch is good, with local cuisine given a gourmet twist, good fish and international dishes. Dinner is romantic with candles on the tables and background music. Also at Devon House are a reasonably priced snack bar and delicious ice cream at I Scream.

$$$ Red Bones Blues Café, 1 Argyle Rd, Kingston 10, T978 8262, www.redbones bluescafe.com. Mon-Fri 1200-2300, Sat 1800-2300. 'Nouvelle Jamaican cuisine', quite expensive but lovely garden and blues music, indoor or outdoor seating in small rooms and sections for intimacy, live music on stage in garden under ackee trees, unless it rains. Beside the music theme they also host art exhibitions, film, theatre, poetry readings and world music. Good service and a good night out.

$$$ The Terrace at Liguanea Club, Knutsford Blvd, T929 0106. Lunch and dinner. Tables outside in the shade of a mango tree, elegant place settings with white linen and prompt, courteous service. Excellent food, high-class Jamaican dishes and very good value. Reservations advised as it is popular with the business crowd at lunch and eminently preferable to the restaurants in the hotels for dinner.

$$$-$$ Saffron Indian Cuisine, Shop 37 Market Pl, 67 Constant Spring Rd, T926 6598, www.tamarindindiancuisine.com. Tue-Sat 1130-2130, Sun 1430-2130.

Same Indian/Asian cuisine as at Tamarind, but with a more formal restaurant and well-stocked bar.

$$$-$$ Tamarind Indian Cuisine, Shop 28, Orchid Plaza, 18-22 Barbican Rd, T977 0695, www.tamarindindiancuisine.com. Mon-Sat 1130-1530, 1730-2130, Sun 1730-2130. Very good Indian restaurant with Asian fusion dishes. They have specialist chefs for Indian, Chinese or kebabs. A good selection of all the usual favourites, popular, so reservations advised at night.

$$ Tea Tree Creperie, 8 Hillcrest Av, Kingston 6, T927 8733, www.teatree creperie.com. Mon-Fri 0800-1900, Sat 1000-1900, Sun 1000-1600. A café and crêperie that takes its teas very seriously, with a good variety of Indian, Sri Lankan, Chinese and Japanese black, green or white teas as well as herbal teas and red bush, while all its coffee is Blue Mountain. The cold drinks are good too, try the frozen mint lemonade on a hot day. Sweet and savoury crêpes make a good lunch but there are also quiches, cakes, soup and salad.

$$-$ Devon House Bakery, Devon House, 26 Hope Rd, Kingston 10. In the converted stable complex behind the Great House, the place to come for gourmet patties for lunch: spicy shrimp, fish, chicken, beef, soy, followed by fresh doughnuts, cheesecake, rum cake, pastries, or go to I Scream for 1 or 2 of their many flavours of ice cream.

$$-$ Scotchie's Jerk Pork Centre, Chelsea Av, Kingston 10. Jerk chicken and pork with festivals, popular with locals. Portions aren't large but the food is authentic. Huge barbecue pits cooking chicken, pork and fish. Go easy with the jerk sauce, which is left to individual discretion.

🔊 Bars and clubs

Kingston *p24, maps p26 and p32*
Most hotels have dancing at weekends. Unless with Jamaican friends, tourists are strongly advised not to probe too deeply into real Jamaican nightlife. The *Jamaica*

Vacation Guide (at hotels, tourist offices) has the latest information. There is always a party going on every weekend in Kingston, and almost every night during any of the holiday seasons. The fliers are well circulated and the light posts full of billboards promoting the respective parties, informing the public of dates and venues. These parties boast loud, lively music from mostly Jamaican and North American culture, with some carrying themes. The gates of the venue usually open around 2200, although the locals don't arrive until about midnight, and the fun stops around 0400. Costs vary, depending on whether drinks are included, but women frequently get in free or for reduced rates, while men have to pay US$10-25.

Bin 26 Wine Bar, Devon House, 26 Hope Rd, Kingston 10, T908 1322. A good mix of clientele, locals and foreigners of all ages, reflecting the variety of wines and prices on offer, a pleasant ambience as with all the Devon House entertainment. Also good light meals and snacks to accompany the wine.

Club Privilege, 14-16 Trinidad Terr, Kingston 5, T622 6532, see Facebook. Thu-Sat 2200-0400. Smart dress code at this club, lots of ladies free nights, free shots nights, etc. The DJ plays a mix of 90s and more recent music, all styles.

Cuddy'z, Shops 4-6, New Kingston Shopping Centre, Kingston 5, T920 8956. Mon-Thu 1130-2300, Fri-Sat 1130-0100, Sun 1800-2300, happy hour 1700-2000. Sports bar owned by former West Indies bowler Courtney Walsh, TVs everywhere, computers on the tables, long modern bar. Food ranges from saltfish and ackee to chicken quesadillas, good callaloo dunk, dishes named after Jamaican sports heroes. Fri nights lots of events. Favourite spot for sports personalities and fans.

Escape 24/7, Knutsford Blvd. A small open-air bar during the day and early evening when you can enjoy laid back drinks with friends and a game of dominoes is transformed from 2300 when the clubbers arrive, best Fri, Sat nights, other nights

quieter. The music is mainly dancehall and hip hop. Ladies free.

Famous, Portmore, T9888801, see Facebook. Thu-Sat 2200-0400. The newest club on the scene, opened in 2013 and drawing people out to Portmore to see what the fuss is all about. Regular ladies' nights with cut-price or free entry, otherwise around US$10, activities advertised on Facebook.

Fiction Lounge, 67 Constant Spring Rd, Kingston 10, T631 8038, www.fiction loungeja.com. A club with an outdoor dance floor. Calls itself Ultra Inclusive and charges US$20 for women, US£25 for men, including all drinks to keep you partying until dawn, but there isn't a huge selection.

Macau Gaming Lounge & Bar, 28 Lindsay Crescent, Kingston 10, T925 6395. Open 1700-0200. A traditional bar with an open-air beach-style area. Best to go in a group to make your own entertainment, not much fun for a couple.

Priscilla's Night Club, 103 Constant Spring Rd, Kingston 8, T931 5073. Favourite for after-work professionals, laid-back atmosphere and great city views. Mostly R&B music, also a Latin night.

The Quad, 20-22 Trinidad Terr, New Kingston, Kingston 5, T754 7823. Jamaica's only multi-level night club, each with its own atmosphere and type of music. Fri and Sat nights are good, while Thu is Hookah night with flavoured vodka on the top floor:

Rae Town, just east of downtown Kingston, is primarily a fishing community on the coast, but it is a very popular inner-city hangout for locals and visitors, on Sun nights, offering a secure experience of street dance urban entertainment 'ghetto style', with typically heavy Dancehall music and reggae from huge sound systems, and a variety of Jamaican food and drink from roadside bars and restaurants.

Spanish Court Rooftop Bar, 1 St Lucia Av, Kingston 5, T926 0000, www.spanishcourt hotel.com. In one of the best hotels in the city, this is a chic after-work bar with good special cocktails and tasty bar snacks,

What to buy, what not to buy

In the craft markets and stores you can find items of wood (by Rastafarians, Maroons and other craftsmen), straw, batik (from a number of good textile companies) and embroidery; the hand-knitted woollen gold, red, green Rasta caps (with or without black dreadlocks affixed) are very cheap. Blue Mountain coffee is excellent, cheaper at airport duty-free shops than in supermarkets or tourist shops.

Check with legislation (and your conscience) before buying articles made from tortoiseshell or crocodile skin, and certain corals, shells and butterflies. Many of these creatures are protected and should not be bought as souvenirs. It is illegal to take or possess black or white coral in Jamaica; sea turtles are protected and you should refuse to buy products made from their shells.

popular with a mixed local and foreign crowd, not just hotel guests.
Usain Bolt's Tracks & Records, The Market Place, 67 Constant Spring Rd, T906 3903, www.tracksandrecords.com. The place to come, whether for food, a drink or just entertainment. There are lots of different areas including a VIP area and mezzanine, the dining area seats 200 (**$$$**). The theme of sports and music, reflected in the name, is highlighted by the 45 flatscreens around and there's always something going on. Also a shop for Bolt merchandise.

🎭 Entertainment

Kingston *p24, maps p26 and p32*
Cinema
Carib Cinema, in the heart of Crossroads, Kingston 5, T926 6106.
The Cineplex, in Sovereign Centre, Shop 47a, 106 Hope Rd, Kingston 6, T978 3522.

Theatre and dance
Edna Manley School for the Visual and Performing Arts produces graduates of a very high standard in art, music and dance. There are several very active theatre and dance companies such as the **Ashe Creative Arts** group, **Dance Theatre Xaymaca**, the **Wolmer's Dance Troupe** and **Praise Academy of Dance Troupe**. **National Dance Theatre Company** is well known internationally. All have shows annually or biannually.

The Barn Theatre, 5 Oxford Rd, Kingston 5, T926 6469.
The Center Stage Theatre, 18 Dominica Dr, Kingston 5, T968 7529.
Little Theatre Movement, 4 Tom Redcam Av, Kingston 5, T926 6129.
The Pantry Playhouse and Dinner Theatre, 2 Dumfries Rd, Kingston 10, T960 9845.
Phillip Sherlock Centre for the Creative Arts (PSCCA), on the grounds of the University of the West Indies, Mona, Kingston 7, T927 1047. Watch the press for details of performances.
Ward Theatre Foundation, North Parade, T922 0453.

🛍 Shopping

Kingston *p24, maps p26 and p32*
Most shops are in the plazas along Constant Spring Rd, in Manor Park and in Liguanea. There is a smart shopping centre in New Kingston with duty-free concessions for visitors.

Arts and crafts
Jamaica Crafts Market, downtown Kingston, at the corner of Ocean Blvd and Port Royal St and many shops at west end of Port Royal St have local crafts. The market is a must for souvenir hunters, craft items are reasonably priced and there is a wide range of traditional Jamaican handicrafts.

Other shops for great local crafts are the **Craft Cottage Limited**, in the Village Plaza, 24 Constant Spring Rd, Kingston 10, T926 0719, **Carby's Craft Village** and **Souvenirs Discount Centre**, shop 4, Twin Gates Plaza, 25 ½ Constant Spring Rd, Kingston 10, T926 4065. **Chelsea Galleries**, Chelsea Rd, **Gallery 14**, **Old Boulevard Gallery**, **Grosvenor Galleries**, 1 Grosvenor Terr, Kingston 8, T924 6684, **Contemporary Art Gallery**, 1 Liguanea Av, Kingston 6, T927 9958. **Things Jamaican**, Devon House, 26 Hope Rd, Kingston 10, T926 1961, and also at both the Norman Manley International Airport in Kingston, T924 8556, and the Donald Sangster International Airport in Montego Bay, T971 0775.

Market
The market off West Queen St is an interesting local market, selling fish, fruit and general produce. Downtown is where Jamaicans shop for bargains, but be careful, particularly in the market, it can be dangerous, even if you don't get robbed.

⚠ What to do

Kingston *p24, maps p26 and p32*
For diving and fishing, see page 75.

Golf
The Constant Spring Golf Club, 152 Constant Spring Rd, Kingston 8, T924 1610. Daily 0800-2200. Built in 1920, glorious view from the 13th tee. 18 holes, green fee US$38 weekdays and US$46 weekends and public holidays. Good clubhouse with sociable bar and pool.
Caymanas Golf Club, Mandela Highway, T922 3388, www.caymanasgolfclub.com. Dates from 1957 and is probably the best in the country. 18 holes, green fee US$42 weekdays and US$54 weekends, Mon-Fri 0830-1600, Sat-Sun 0630-1630; golf cart rental US$23 and US$15.50 for the caddy. There is also a pro shop, a restaurant, 2 bars and a pool.

The Jamaica Golf Association, Constant Spring Rd, Kingston 8, T925 2325, jamaicagolf@cwjamaica.com. Has information on tournaments.
Putt 'n' Play Mini Golf Park, 78 Knutsford Blvd, Kingston 5, T906 4814. Mon-Fri 1700-2300, Sat-Sun 1700-2400. 18 holes and an artificial turf with streams and bridges, sand patches, and greens, giving players a real golf experience. There are instructors on hand to give lessons or pointers. The environment is very relaxed with a snack bar, lounge chairs, a pool table and background music. There are also rides for children which operate on Sat and Sun until 2200, good family night out.

Spectator sports
Basketball has become increasingly popular in Jamaica over the last decade, with the sport becoming more and more competitive and exciting each year. Contact the **Jamaica Basketball Association**, and get information on the newly formed and very popular National Basketball League (NBL), as well as the Division 2 League, and the Women's League.
Cricket is the island's main spectator sport, although it was temporarily overtaken by football (soccer) in 1998 when Jamaica qualified for the World Cup. Test matches are played at Sabina Park. For details on matches ring **Jamaica Cricket Association**, George Headley Stand, Sabina Park, Kingston 4, T967 0322, www.cricketjamaica.org.
Football For information on national team matches as well as the very popular National Premier League matches, contact the **Jamaica Football Federation**, 20 St Lucia Crescent, Kingston 5, T754 7976-8.
Horse racing At Caymanas Park, T704 5042, every Wed and Sat and most public holidays.
Polo International tournaments are held at **Caymanas Polo Club**.

Tennis

Try the **Eric Bell Tennis Centre**. For tennis development and youth training in Jamaica, see Tennis Jamaica, T906 5700, www.facebook.com/tennisjamaica.

Tour operators

Sun Venture Tours, 30 Balmoral Av, Kingston 10, T960 6685, SunVenture ToursLimited on Facebook. Activities for nature lovers away from the beach, hiking, caving, safaris, birdwatching, downhill Blue Mountain bicycle tours and educational tours, managed by Robert Kerr.

⊖ Transport

Kingston *p24, maps p26 and p32*
Bus

Fares from Kingston with Knutsford Express, T971 1822, www.knutsfordexpress.com, are: US$16 to **Mandeville**, US$24.50 to **Montego Bay**, US$27 to **Negril**, US$16 to **Ocho Rios**. The bus leaves from 18 Dominica Dr, entrance on Grenada Cres opposite New Kingston Shopping Centre.

The local Government bus service, **Jamaica Urban Transit Company** (JUTC), has well marked buses with destinations and numbers, US$1 for adults, students in uniform, children, the disabled and pensioners pay half price, unless they have a Smart Card, in which case fares are US$0.20. To get to New Kingston by bus, change bus (to No 83) downtown. The recognized service between town and airport is JUTA, taxi/minibus, which charges US$21 to New Kingston (taxi dispatcher gives you a note of fare before you leave, can be shared).

Taxi

Taxis have red licence plates with PP/PPV (Public Passenger Vehicle) on them. They are usually available at the airport if a large plane has landed, and are cheaper, at US$20 to Kingston, depending on destination, than the **JUTA** (Jamaica Union of Travellers Association, T927 4534, www.jutatoursjamaica.com) transfers by shared van.

Blue Mountains and the east

The Blue Mountains are synonymous with the greatest coffee in the world, sold at premium prices because of its exquisite flavour acquired during its slow growth on the cool, misty slopes where methods of cultivation, harvesting and roasting are the same as they have been for 200 years. It is also the most beautiful part of Jamaica, with forests, trails, birds and flowers for all nature lovers and the hike up to the highest point, Middle Peak, to see the dawn inspires a huge sense of achievement and wonder. It has been nominated as a UNESCO World Heritage Site. The coast around Port Antonio is also attractive and unspoilt, being quite a distance from either of the main airports. Pretty bays, sandy coves, banana plantations, waterfalls and rafting on the Rio Grande characterize this end of the island.

North from Kingston → *For listings, see pages 53-55.*

Behind Kingston lie the **Blue Mountains**, with Blue Mountain Peak rising to a height of 2256 m. This is undoubtedly one of the most spectacular and beautiful parts of Jamaica and an absolute must for keen birdwatchers and botanists and also for those who like hiking.

Papine to Newcastle
It is possible to explore some of the Blue Mountains by ordinary car from Kingston via Papine. After leaving Papine and just after passing the **Blue Mountain Inn** (good restaurant), turn left to Irish Town and on to **Newcastle**, a Jamaica Defence Force training camp at 1219 m with magnificent views of Kingston and Port Royal. The road goes right through the parade grounds, where you can often see troops training as you drive past. There are still the insignias of the various British regiments stationed here before independence and the cannon brought from Port Royal in 1906 for training purposes. The British moved up to Newcastle and the surrounding area called Red Light to escape yellow fever and the heat of the capital.

The road to **Catherine's Peak** (1585 m) directly behind the camp is about an hour's climb for the moderately fit.

Blue and John Crow Mountains National Park
ⓘ *Managed by the Jamaica Conservation and Development Trust (JCDT), 29 Dumbarton Av, Kingston 10, T9208278, www.jcdt.org.jm, or www.blueandjohncrowmountains.org.*
The Blue and John Crow Mountain National Park (BJCMNP) encompasses 78,212 ha of mountains, forests and rivers and is composed of three ranges, Port Royal, Blue and John Crow Mountains which are divided by the Buff Bay and Rio Grande valleys. The park contains

Jamaican flora and fauna

The 'land of wood and water' is a botanist's paradise. There are reported to be about 3000 species of flowering plants, 827 of which are not found anywhere else. There are over 550 varieties of fern, 300 of which can be found in **Fern Gully**. There are many orchids, bougainvillea, hibiscus and other tropical flowers. Tropical hardwoods like cedar and mahogany, palms, balsa and many other trees, besides those that are cultivated, can be seen. Cultivation, however, is putting much of Jamaica's plant life at risk. Having been almost entirely forested, an estimated 6% of the land is virgin forest. A great many species are endangered.

This is also a land of hummingbirds and butterflies (see page 49). Sea cows and the Pedro seal are found in the island's waters, although fewer than 100 sea cows, or manatee, survive. There are crocodiles, but no large wild mammals apart from the hutia, or coney (an endangered species), the mongoose (considered a pest since it eats chickens) and, in the mountains, wild boar. There are, however, lots of bats, with 25 species recorded. Most live in caves or woods and eat fruit and insects, but there is a fish-eating bat which can sometimes be seen swooping over the water in Kingston Harbour. The Jamaican iguana (*Cyclura collei*) was thought to have died

out in the 1960s, but in 1990 a small group was found to be surviving in the Hellshire Hills. There are six species of snake, all harmless and rare, the largest of which is the yellow snake (the Jamaican boa), which can grow up to 3 m.

Good sites for birdwatching are given in the text; the three main areas are the **Cockpit Country**, the **Blue Mountains** and **Marshall's Pen**. The national bird is the red-billed streamertail hummingbird (*Trochilus polytmus*), also known as the doctor bird or swallow tail hummingbird. The male has a long, sweeping tail much longer than its body, and is one of Jamaica's endemic species. Other endemic birds are the yellow-billed parrot and the black-billed parrot, found in the Cockpit Country or Hope Zoo. There are 25 species and 21 subspecies of endemic land birds which are found nowhere else. A good place to see Jamaica's birds is the **Rocklands Feeding Station**, near Montego Bay. On weekday evenings you can watch the birds being fed and even offer a hummingbird a syrup and get really close. Many migratory birds stop on Jamaica on their journeys north or south. One of the best references is *Birds of Jamaica: a photographic field guide* by Audrey Downer and Robert Sutton with photos by Yves-Jacques Rey Millet Cambridge University Press (1990).

the largest area of natural forest on Jamaica. Its core area, about half of the total, has great biological diversity. Here you can find the national bird, the streamertail hummingbird, also known as the doctor bird, and the giant swallowtail butterfly, the largest in the Western Hemisphere. The remainder is either degraded forest, or Caribbean pine plantations and land given over to coffee cultivation. This zone is designated for sustainable use, while a buffer zone is being developed for the provision of sustainable livelihoods for local people.

Holywell Recreation Area

① *US$5, children US$2, Jamaicans J$100. Oately Mountain Trail is a commercial trail within the Holywell Park for which there is a separate user fee of US$5, including guided tour (check when booking that a guide is available). Bookings can be made through the JCDT, as above.*

Beyond Newcastle lie **Hardwar Gap** and **Holywell Recreation Area**, within the Blue and John Crow Mountains National Park. Holywell offers nature trails, three fully-equipped cabins for rent, which cost US$50 or US$70, camping at US$5 per night and picnic areas.

The picturesque little community of **Section** is an old Maroon lookout point at the junction of three roads and is a travel halt. There the road from Holywell intersects with the Silver Hill to Buff Bay Road. A left turn takes you to Buff Bay and a turning off to the right to Silver Hill Gap. The road from Section to Buff Bay is prone to landslides and blockages so before setting out make enquiries about the road. Section is the most popular spot on the north side of the Blue Mountains for purchasing genuine Blue Mountain coffee. A coffee tour is offered which includes a demonstration of the traditional way of growing, preparing and roasting Blue Mountain coffee, as it has been done for 200 years.

The Old Tavern Coffee Estate ① *T924 2785*, run by Dorothy Twyman (widow of the founder, Alex Twyman) and her son, David, is a small family farm on the cool, northern slopes of the Blue Mountains where coffee is grown at about 1200 m and considered by many connoisseurs to be the finest in the world. They get some 150 ins/450 cm of rain a year, lots of cloud and very little sunshine, so the coffee takes 10 months to develop from blossom to picking, compared with four months in other coffee-growing areas around the world. The bean is harder, bigger and contains more sugars as a result. Once picked, the beans have to be taken to Kingston for drying in the sun. The tour is free, but you are unlikely to leave without buying some of their delicious, freshly-roasted coffee. This is also the place to come for the peaberry coffee bean. The single bean is much prized by connoisseurs and here they are picked out from the rest of the crop and sold separately. The whole enterprise is a very labour-intensive business.

The road from Silver Hill Gap goes to the left turn-off to Clydesdale (about a 4-km drive). The road to Clydesdale and beyond, to the **Cinchona Botanical Garden** is unpaved and very steep between Clydesdale and Cinchona (4WD required, or walk, about two hours uphill but well worth it). The route from Silver Hill Gap continues past the turn-off to Clydesdale to **Content Gap**. Content is a three-road junction; coming from Clydesdale the right turn goes to Gordon Town and Kingston whereas the left goes to Mavis Bank and Blue Mountain Peak.

At **Mavis Bank** you have the opportunity to tour another Blue Mountain coffee enterprise, this one on a different scale. The **Mavis Bank Coffee Factory** (MBCF) ① *entrance off the road from Gordon Town as you reach the village, T977 8013, Mon-Fri 0830-1200, 1300-1530, US$8, children US$3.50, reservations advised*, has been in operation since 1923 and is the largest coffee factory in Jamaica. It is supplied by some 5000 small farms, including its own six plantations, and employs over 300 people. The coffee berries are picked by hand, then left in the sun to dry (barbecue) for five to seven days, unless it is too wet, in which case they are artificially dried in a big tumble drier. The beans then mature in big sacks, are hulled, cleaned and finally roasted to make the famous Jablum coffee. The whole process takes over four months before the coffee is ready to be exported in barrels. Although the factory was originally established by an English planter, Victor Munn, it is now 70% owned by the National Investment Bank of Japan (NIJB), with the Munn family owning the remaining shares. The Japanese relationship is reflected in sales as over three quarters of MBCF coffee is consumed in Japan, the rest going to the USA, Europe and the rest of the world.

Blue Mountain

To go towards Blue Mountain Peak from Kingston (Corporate Area) via Papine, drive straight on at **Blue Mountain Inn** (instead of turning left), through Gordon Town and on through **Mavis Bank** to **Hagley Gap**, if the Mahogany Vale ford is passable. The community and the national park have constructed a flat bridge that has made passage more secure even during the rainy season. However, you will almost certainly not be able to get a car up to the starting point for the walk to the peak. Public transport up the Blue Mountains is infrequent. There are some buses to Mavis Bank from the square in Papine, US$1, or route taxis for around US$2.50, but you will need to ask. Taxis from Kingston to Mavis Bank are about US$25-30. Only 4WD vehicles are advisable after Mavis Bank (no shortage of people offering to take you), and there are no petrol stations en route. There are two options for getting to the start of the trail at Penlynecastle/Abbey Green area: walking from Mavis Bank to Penlynecastle, or taking a 4WD. The two hiking routes are the short cut (4.5 km uphill through villages), or along the road from Mavis Bank (6.5 km to Hagley Gap, then 4 km to Penlynecastle). A guide is recommended for both options but especially if taking the short cut. Local guides are available and the Mavis Bank Police are always willing to assist in locating one. Ask for **Whitfield Hall** or **Wildflower Lodge**, the turning is just beyond Penlynecastle School, by the post office. From Penlynecastle it's 3.2 km to Abbey Green. This is the last part that can be done by vehicle. Transport is available from **Whitfield Hall**, a coffee farm which offers basic lodging, camping and breakfast for hikers before they set out on the trail to the peak, and **Wildflower Lodge**, which also offers lodging (see Where to stay, below). After Abbey Green there is a 3.7-km hike uphill to the ranger station at **Portland Gap**, which has bunk rooms (US$23-35), rooms with floor space (US$14.50) and camping facilities (US$2 per person). **Sun Venture Tours** (see page 43) provide complete tour services for Blue Mountain Peak, with transfers from anywhere on the island to Penlynecastle, meals, accommodation and guides.

Climbing the peak The Blue Mountains play a symbolic role for Jamaicans. Jamaican poet Roger Mais (1905-1955) wrote a moving poem called *All Men Come to the Hills* about men's desire to rest finally in the hills, wherever or however they have spent their lives. The walk to **Blue Mountain Peak** from Whitfield Hall or Wildflower Lodge (about 10 km) takes three to four hours up and two to three hours down. If you stay the night at Portland Gap, it's 5.6 km to the summit. All hikers have to pay US$5 to use the trail (Jamaicans J$200), payable at the JCDT office (see page 44) or at Portland Gap ranger station.

The first part, called **Jacob's Ladder**, is the steepest and leads to Portland Gap. Some start very early in the morning in the hope of watching the sunrise from the peak. The thrill of victory takes on new meaning once you've climbed Jacob's Ladder and posed atop the Trig Station on the highest point, **Middle Peak** (2256 m), waiting anxiously ... braving the bitter cold ... to catch that first faint glow of sunlight. As often as not, though, the peak is shrouded in cloud and rain in the early morning; a disheartening experience. You can leave in early daylight and almost certainly reach the top before it starts clouding over again (mid to late morning). In this case you do not need a guide, as the path is straightforward. Short cuts should be avoided at all costs. The trail winds through a fascinating variety of vegetation: coffee groves and banana plantations on the lower, south slopes, to tree ferns and dwarf forest near the summit (with some explanatory and mileage signposts). The doctor bird – a beautiful swallow-tailed hummingbird, the national bird of Jamaica – is fairly common. It's quite hard to spot, at first recognizable by its loud buzz, especially near the many flowering bushes. Take your own food and torch (spare set of batteries and bulb), sweater and raincoat if you set out in the darkness. At holiday times, especially in the summer, scores of people walk up Blue Mountain Peak every day, while in low season there will be only a handful. Considering the numbers, it is remarkably unspoiled and the views are spectacular.

Another trail, to **Mossman Peak**, starts at Portland Gap, but is not included in the national park's recreational areas.

Leaving Kingston

The A4 road runs east out of Kingston, all along the south coast through Bull Bay, Yallahs, Morant Bay and Port Morant, before turning up on to the north coast to Port Antonio, Buff Bay and Annotto Bay, where it ends at the junction with the A3 running directly north from Kingston. Just beyond **Bull Bay** on the way to Yallahs, there is a plaque in memory of '**Three-Finger Jack**', Jack Mansong, one of Jamaica's legendary highway men and a folk hero-villain in the mould of Robin Hood. From the marker you get a magnificent view of Kingston harbour to the southwest, while to the north are the dry forested hills of the Port Royal Mountains, once the territory of Jack. He fought a guerrilla war single-handedly against the British military and the plantocracy. It is not known whether he was born in Africa or Jamaica in 1780-1781. He is thought to have lost two fingers in a battle with a maroon called Quashie who later killed Jack in another fight, whereupon he cut off his head and three remaining fingers as trophies. Legends about Jack proliferated, books about him became popular and then came a musical, or pantomime. *Obi-* or *Three-Fingered Jack* had a run of some nine years at the Covent Garden, Haymarket and Victoria Theatres in London. (Further reading: L Alan Eyre, *Jack Mansong, 'Bloodshed or Brotherhood'*.)

Albion Great House and Aqueduct

About 300 m from the junction of the A4 with the roads to Easington and Yallahs at Albion are the overgrown ruins of the Albion Great House and Aqueduct, often referred to as **Albion Castle**. Of the remaining structures the great house and the waterwheel are the most impressive. Descendants of those who worked on the estate as slaves still occupy the 'slave house' today. In colonial times the estate was the leading producer of sugar in Jamaica and its crystal sugar was known as 'Albion Sugar'. On emancipation in 1838 there were about 450 slaves at Albion producing 400 hogsheads of sugar and more than double that quantity of rum was being produced at the end of the century. Its waterwheels were supplied by a large aqueduct transporting water from the Yallahs River several kilometres away. One of the wheels had a diameter of 9.6 m and supported 88 buckets. These and other innovations in the milling and drying process made Albion Estate a leader in sugar production technology. The estate was sold off in small lots to farmers to try and prevent urban migration, but is now mostly housing with convenient access to Kingston. Without the extensive irrigation system, the land has reverted to its natural dry state.

Yallahs

Yallahs is one of the major towns in St Thomas. No one is quite sure where the town got its name, but it may have been named after a privateer, or buccaneer, called Captain Yhallahs, who operated in the area around 1671. On the other hand it may have been a corruption of Hato de Ayala, the name of one of the large cattle ranches run by the Spanish when they occupied the island. **Yallahs Ponds** stretch for about 5 km, providing an outstanding landmark. Legend has it that two brothers argued over the sub-division of a piece of land and the argument became so fierce that the two plots of land sank, forming two of the three salt ponds. The hyper-saline ponds created a unique ecosystem and several scientific discoveries have been made here. The bacteria in the ponds made them extremely smelly and in 1902 it was so bad that people in Kingston were complaining. Channels were made between the ponds and out to the sea, which solved the problem and the smell has not been so bad since. The ponds are also good spots for birdwatching. Local people used to harvest the salt and sell it for pickling and preserving mackerel or pork. However, a few years ago the salt in one of the ponds ceased to appear. It would come up with the water in the wet season and then as the water receded the salt would be left behind for people to gather, but now the water is fresh and there is no salt. A 4WD vehicle is recommended for visiting the beach side of the ponds, ask directions in town, best at **Miss Johnson's A&I Bar and Restaurant** in the centre, or contact the **Yallahs Community Development Fund** ① *T982 5021/706 3035*. The dumping of wrecked cars spoils the first part of the journey but beyond that it is great going.

Morant Bay

Morant Bay, the capital of St Thomas, has a colourful and legendary past. On 11 October 1865, it was the scene of the Morant Bay Rebellion. A group of farmers and other disaffected citizens led by farmer and Baptist Deacon, Paul Bogle, marched to the Courthouse to complain about high taxes, the collapse of the sugar industry and the economic downturn, which had been exacerbated by drought and outbreaks of smallpox and cholera. The Government was not sympathetic to the views of the people, the Courthouse was burned down and the uprising assumed dangerous proportions. The military rounded up the protestors and killed or sentenced to death hundreds of men and women who had allegedly taken part, burned nearly 1000 homes and flogged members of the surrounding communities. The replacement Courthouse burned down again in 2007.

Bath and nearby treks

North of Port Morant at the east end of the island, is Bath, another place from which to access the **John Crow Mountains** (named after the ubiquitous turkey buzzards). There is a modest hotel, **Bath Fountain Hotel and Spa**, dating from 1727, where the main attraction is the natural **hot water spring baths** ① *T703 4345, bathmineralspahotelja@ yahoo.com, overnight stays ($$$) include 20-min mineral bath*, which are most relaxing at the end of a long day. Outside the hotel there is competition from locals offering showers and massages further up the river. There are also stalls selling treatments, drinks, etc. Two passes above Bath, the **Cuna Cuna Pass** and the **Cornpuss Gap** lead down to the source of the Rio Grande River on the north slopes of the mountain range. Both are tough treks, particularly the Cornpuss Gap. It is absolutely essential to take a local guide. The north slopes of the mountain range are the home of the unique and extremely rare **Jamaican butterfly**, *Papilio homerus*, a large black and yellow swallowtail. It is the second-largest butterfly in the world and the largest in the Americas, and is protected under international law (CITES) regulating the trade in endangered species. This butterfly is very spectacular in flight and easily recognizable because of its size. It can best be seen in May and June.

Pera Beach to Long Bay

East of Port Morant, but not easily accessible, is the magnificent **Pera Beach** on the south coast between Port Morant and Morant Lighthouse. The lighthouse, built 1841, is at the far eastern tip of the island and is a National Heritage Monument (www.jnht.com). There are great views from the top. Nearby are remote beaches in Holland Bay. Just before reaching Manchioneal a road off to the left leads to the **Reach Falls** ① *about 3.5 km, Wed-Sun 0830-1630, US$10, Jamaicans J$300, children half price*. Well worth a visit if you have a car or are prepared to walk (45 minutes with views of rolling forested hills) from the main road. Pretty tiers of smooth boulders and one major waterfall of about 4.5 m tumble through a lush, green gorge into a pool where you can swim. Guides can lead walks above the fall. The government manages the Falls and there are toilets and changing facilities. Buses from main road to Port Antonio are infrequent, every one or two hours. Taxis are a better option and more frequent. Further along the coast from Manchioneal is **Long Bay**, which, as the name suggests, is an extensive stretch of gorgeous pale sand. Tides can be strong so check conditions before swimming. Beach bars, cottages and guesthouses have been built on the beach. The land behind the beach has been replanted with coconut palms after disease killed off the plantations. Old tree trunks are not taken down but left for woodpeckers, owls and hawks.

Port Antonio → *For listings, see pages 53-55.*

Once the major banana port, where many of the island's first tourists arrived on banana boats, Port Antonio dates back to the 16th century. Built on the back of sugar cane plantations and the export of sugar, by the mid-19th century the numbers of plantations had dwindled and by the end of the century sugar had died out. The land was divided up into smaller plots for peasant farmers to grow ground provisions and it was they who began to grow bananas. By the 1870s, the export of bananas became a profitable business and planting began in earnest. Within a few decades the wharves and warehouses were full of green bananas and Port Antonio became the world's banana capital, made famous in Harry Belafonte's 'Banana Boat Song'. An enterprising trader, Captain Baker, decided to fill his boats on the return journey from the USA with people seeking to escape the cold winters on the eastern seaboard and the first tourists arrived. He built the first hotel in 1905. You can still see bananas loaded at Boundbrook Wharf, but there are no longer lines of men passing the bunches from head to head, as these are all packaged and loaded by machines. Disease and hurricanes wreaked havoc on the banana industry, and the multinational companies who had taken it over have now left and bananas are back in the hands of small growers.

Places in Port Antonio
Port Antonio's prosperity has for many years been in gentle decline and it is now run-down, but it has an atmosphere unlike any other town in Jamaica, with some superb old public buildings. It is an excellent base from which to explore inland or along the coast. The **tourist office** ① *upstairs in City Centre Plaza on Harbour St, T993 3051*, is quite helpful, with timetables for local buses ('soon come'), which leave regularly when full, but at uncertain hours, from the seafront behind the Texaco station. See also www.portantoniotravel.com.

The oldest part of town is on the headland between the two bays, West Harbour and East Harbour, which offer natural harbours. Called **The Hill**, it is where the wealthy merchants used to live, away from the noise and smells of the port. The British called it Titchfield after the estate of the Duke of Portland in England, with **Upper Titchfield** where the posh people lived and **Lower Titchfield** where the workers lived along the sea front. Despite the decay, you can still imagine the grandeur of life in colonial times in the rusting ironwork and rotting wooden fretwork. **De Montevin Lodge** is a fine example of how pretty the houses used to be. You can see the remains of **Fort George**, built on the bluff from 1729 onwards to deter a Spanish invasion, but the barracks and parade ground are now the class rooms and sports ground for Titchfield School.

The **town centre** is at the start of the peninsula, overlooking East Harbour. Here you can find a clocktower, the Courthouse, Port Antonio's Parish Church on the seafront, with its sandstone brick and long thin windows, and a weird shopping mall designed using the architectural styles of several European countries from different centuries, quite a mish-mash.

East of town are **Frenchman's Cove** and **San San**, both beautiful private beaches, which you can get to after paying an entrance fee. At the **Blue Lagoon** (also known as the Blue Hole), a fresh-water spring meets a coastal inlet to create another beauty spot of turquoise waters surrounded by green trees. According to local legend it is bottomless, but since Jacques Cousteau dived it, it is measured at 57 m. It was the setting for the Brooke Shields film of the same name and has been declared a National Heritage site. You can swim and there are bamboo raft and other boat trips; facilities are undergoing renovation. Next along the coast is **Fairy Hill Beach**, also known as Winnefred Beach, and then **Boston Bay** renowned for its local jerk food pits; several unnamed places by the roadside serve hot spicy chicken, pork or fish, chopped up and wrapped in paper, cooked on planks over a pit of hot coals, very good and tasty.

Around Port Antonio → *For listings, see pages 53-55.*

Somerset Falls
ⓘ *T873 1198, daily 0900-1700, US$12.*
To get here take a bus towards Buff Bay (any westbound Kingston bus), get out at the sign about 15 km from Port Antonio and walk for five minutes. You can hike along trails, swim in the pools and take a boat ride into a cave behind the falls, set in a deep gorge covered in rainforest. Food and drink is available and there are toilets.

Folly Ruins
About 30 minutes' walk east around the bay from Port Antonio are the Folly Ruins, an elaborate, turn-of-the-century mansion built in the style of Roman and Greek architecture, now in ruins (partly because the millionaire American's wife took an instant dislike to it). It is a ghostly, crumbling old mansion in an open field with lovely views shared with grazing cows. To find it, fork right off the path before going into a clump of trees on the peninsula (leading towards the lighthouse inside the military camp).

Nonsuch Cave
ⓘ *Daily 0900-1600, US$6, call T993 3740 in advance to check that it is open.*
At Nonsuch Cave, several kilometres to the southeast in the same vicinity as the Athenry Gardens, there are fossils, stalactites and evidence of Taíno occupation in 14 chambers. There's a gift shop and lunch area too, but no public transport.

Navy Island and Errol Flynn Marina
In the harbour is the 28-ha Navy Island, at one time owned by Errol Flynn. There are beaches and there used to be a resort, but none of the facilities are in use at the time of writing. It is awaiting redevelopment and has been for a while. It may be possible to visit but there is no ferry there. The **Errol Flynn Marina** ⓘ *www.errolflynnmarina.com*, opened in 2002 as a world-class yachting centre that can handle every size of boat. It has a restaurant, dive shop, swimming pool and shops, as well as the services required by yachtsmen and women. It is the headquarters of the International Blue Marlin Tournament every October.

Rafting on the Rio Grande

① T913 5433/4, reservations essential, 0900-1700, last raft at 1600, US$72 per raft, takes a couple and child under 10; private captains are cheaper, but they are illegal and have no insurance.

Flynn saw the bamboo rafts which used to bring bananas down the Rio Grande as a potential tourist attraction. If you turn up at Berridale there are now always expert rafters ready and willing to take you down the river. The trip takes 2½ hours (depending on the river flow, it can take four hours, take sunscreen and a hat) through magnificent scenery and there is an opportunity to stop en route. A driver takes your car down from the embarkation point to the point of arrival, **Rafter's Rest**, on the main coastal road (US$30), recommended as a place to have a pleasant, moderately priced lunch or drink, even if you are not proposing to raft. Otherwise, the return taxi fare is US$20; there are also buses back to Berridale, the setting-off point, though infrequent. Returning from St Margaret's, downstream, is easier as there are plenty of buses passing between Annotto Bay and Port Antonio.

The Maroons

The Rio Grande valley is also well worth exploring, including a trip to the Maroons (descendants of escaped slaves) at **Moore Town**, but the roads are rough and public transport minimal. **Grand Valley Tours** *① T993 4116, valleytour@cwjamaica.com, run by Veronica Thaxter, who arranges tours of the town with Colonel Harris, the leader of the Maroons, and is recommended for guided tours, by reservation only. For accommodation call Lynette Wilks, T395 5351, bjcush1@hotmail.com, cabins sleep 3 ($$).* To the west of the Rio Grande lie the north slopes of the Blue Mountains. **Nanny Town**, the home of the Maroons, was destroyed by the British in 1734 and then 'lost' until the 1960s. There is recent archaeological evidence at Nanny Town to suggest that the Maroons originally took to the mountains and lived with (and possibly later absorbed) Taíno peoples. There have been some dramatic discoveries of Taíno wooden carvings which are now on display at the National Gallery.

Port Antonio to Buff Bay

Between Port Antonio and the Buff Bay area there are several roads into the interior from places such as Hope Bay. Just to the east of Buff Bay, near Orange Bay, is **Spring Garden**, and from there the road goes on to Chepstowe and thence to **Claverty Cottage** and **Thompson Gap**; spectacular scenery, waterfalls in the valleys and very remote. It was possible to walk from Thompson Gap over the Blue Mountains via Morces Gap and down to Clydesdale (The Vinegar Hill Trail), but the trails are little used and may not be passable.

Blue Mountains and the east listings

For hotel and restaurant price codes and other relevant information, see pages 12-14.

🛏 Where to stay

Holywell Recreation Area *p45*

$$$$-$$$ Starlight Chalet & Health Spa, T969 3116, Kingston office T960 3070, www.starlightchalet.com. A hideaway in the Blue Mountains, good for relaxing, birdwatching and hiking. Spa, TV, bar and restaurant serving local and international dishes, transport on request, under 11s stay free.

$$ The Gap B&B at **The Gap Café and Gift Shoppe**, T995 3093, details on the Port Antonio Guesthouse Association website, www.go-jam.com. 5 mins' walk from the recreational area, cottage with bedroom, bath and verandah, meals available at the café.

Blue Mountain *p46*
Mountain lodges

$$$$ Lime Tree Farm, Tower Hill, Mavis Bank, T881 8788, www.limetreefarm.com. Charlie and Suzie Burbury run this working coffee farm with glorious views down into Cedar and Yallus valley and across the Blue Mountains. 3 cottages, each individually furnished with a large, comfy bedroom which can sleep a family, bathroom and terrace. Price includes full board and transfers from Kingston. Suzie cooks excellent Jamaican dishes using local ingredients and lots of herbs. Good hiking on nearby trails, friendly staff, internet access, honour bar, environmentally aware, funding for local school and community projects.

$$$$-$$$ Forres Park Guest House, on the main road near the **Mavis Bank Coffee Factory**, T927 8275, www.forrespark.com. Run by the Lyn family. Rooms in main house, a Swiss-style chalet, 4 cabins nearby, all with private bathroom and balcony. In middle of a coffee plantation, excellent birdwatching, many trails for hiking. 4WD transport can be arranged with a guide to the Blue Mountain Peak. The family also owns another coffee farm, **Abbey Green**, higher up at 1500 m, with a small lodge which can be used as a base before hiking up the Peak and for birdwatching.

$$-$ Whitfield Hall Hostel, close to where the Blue Mountain trail begins (the Allgrove family, T879 0514, www.whitfieldhall.com). A large wooden lodge on a coffee farm with no electricity but paraffin lamps, capacity 40, hostel or private room, cold showers only. No meals unless you order them in advance, but kitchen with gas stoves and crockery, for guests' use. Very peaceful and homely with comfortable lounge, log fire and library (visitors' books dating back to the 1950s), friendly and helpful staff. If the hostel is full, camping is permitted.

$$-$ Wildflower Lodge, just before Whitfield Hall, near the start of Blue Mountain trail, known locally as the White House, T929 5394 (or c/o Dudu, Penlynecastle PA, St Thomas). Similar to Whitfield Hall, but a bit more modern, breakfast US$5, evening meals US$7, substantial and excellent vegetables from the garden.

Both lodges will arrange 4WD transport from Mavis Bank (Wildflower Lodge will also arrange transport from Kingston and the airport) and offer guides and mules for walking and carrying bags.

Port Antonio *p50*

Port Antonio has a **Guesthouse Association** offering good-value lodging, excursions and transfers, www.go-jam.com.

$$$$ Goblin Hill Villas at San San, T993 7443, reservations c/o 11 East Av, Kingston 10, T925 8108, www.goblinhill.com. 44 rooms in 1- or 2-bedroomed villas, kitchen, restaurant or housekeepers available, cheaper with no sea view, tennis, short walk to beach, pool, bar, TV room. Also has **Tree Bar**, built around a ficus tree, open 1700-2200.

$$$$ Jamaica Palace, Drapers, T993 7720,www.jamaicapalace.com. 10 mins from Port Antonio, 65 rooms, a/c, beach, pool, wheelchair accessible, watersports.

$$$$ Mocking Bird Hill, Frenchman's Cove, Port Antonio, T993 7134, www.hotel mockingbirdhill.com. 15 mins from town, 5 mins' walk from beach, free shuttle and entry to Frenchman's Cove; 10 rooms in Caribbean-style villa in 3 ha of parkland, pool, gardens, nature trail, restaurant with Jamaican and international cuisine, Carriacou art gallery, wellbeing/massage area, commitment to responsible, local tourism.

$$$$ Trident Villas and Hotel, Anchovy, T993 7000, www.tridentportantonio.com. Refurbished hotel and 13 villas with 1950s-1960s style, sea view, breakfast included, pools, restaurant, spa and gym.

$$$$-$$$ Bay View Eco-Resort & Spa, Anchovy, Port Antonio, T993 3118, www.bayviewecoresort.com. 4 beautiful cottages amidst lush coconut plantation, overlooking Turtle Crawl Harbour; 33 rooms in all, relaxing atmosphere with pool, restaurant and bar, breakfast included, spa offers a variety of treatments.

$$$$-$$$ Jamaica Crest Resort and Villas, Fairy Hill, T993 8400, crest@ discoverjamaica.com. A Christian Resort with 52 luxurious rooms and 14 villas, pool, tennis court, horse riding, restaurant and a lovely view of the sea. They offer a shuttle service to Boston.

$$$$-$$$ Moon San Villa, San San, Drapers, at the Blue Lagoon, T993 7777, www.moonsanvilla.com. A cosy 3-floor villa with 5 bedrooms, complimentary breakfast, and free access to the Blue Lagoon, free use of boat, under same ownership as **Blue Mountain Bicycle Tours**.

$$$$-$$ Great Huts, Boston Beach, T993 8888, www.greathuts.com. An eco-resort with a range of tree houses, garden rooms and rustic huts, good for families, healing centre, cultural programmes, restaurant.

$$$-$$ Demontevin Lodge, 21 Fort George St, Titchfield Hill, T993 2604,

demontevin@cwjamaica.com. Breakfast included, shared bath, more expensive rooms have private bath, old Edwardian house with tiled steps up to the front door, wooden floorboards, restaurant serves set meals, good value.

$$$-$$ Ivanhoe's Guest House, 9 Queen St, T993 3043, ivanhoesja@hotmail.com (www.go-jam.com). Some rooms with shared bath, patio with bay view. Several nearby private houses take guests.

$$ Triff's Inn, 1 Bridge St. Modern, clean, 17 rooms, restaurant, bars.

🍴 Restaurants

Holywell Recreation Area *p45*

$$$ The Gap Café, Hardwar Gap, Newcastle, T997 3032. Long drive but has spectacular views. Breakfast, lunch, high tea and dinner, and serves fresh Blue Mountain coffee. See Where to stay, above.

Port Antonio *p50*

$$$ Bushbar, at the exclusive **Geejam Hotel**, San San, T993 7000, www.geejam hotel.com. Reserve in advance if not staying at the hotel. Beautiful setting overlooking the sea, high-end dining, good music and drinks.

$$$ San San Tropez, Drapers, T993 7213, www.sansantropez.com. Italian restaurant with good pizza, also has villas for rent, good service.

$$ The Best Kept Secret, on road coming into Port Antonio from the west, little blue and yellow shack with banana leaves hanging from it, perched on a cliff, T809 6276. Alvin Dickie Butler and his wife Joy offer dining with beautiful view of Port Antonio, breakfast, lunch and high tea, home cooking, Dickie's famous clientele have included Errol Flynn, the Duke of Edinburgh, Winnie Mandela and Princess Margaret.

$$-$ Anna Banana's, 7 Folly Rd, T715 6533. Beach bar serving Jamaican food throughout the day, specializes in seafood.

$$-$ Woody's Low Bridge Place, on the main road east, between Trident Castle and Frenchman's Cove, T993 7888. Open daily (reservations needed in the evening) for a range of burgers, including vegetarian, and a lot more besides, drinks and music.
$ Coronation Bakery, near Musgrave Market, 18 West St, T993 2710. Good for cheap patties and spice buns as well as bread, rolls, gratto (round bread cut open when hot from oven and stuffed with cheese), bread pudding and rock cakes.
$ Dekal Café, shop 4, City Centre Plaza, T297 7566, Dekal-Internet-Café on Facebook. Sun-Thu 0900-1900, Fri-Sat 0900-2100.

Breakfast, lunches, sandwiches, coffee, desserts and internet.

🎵 Bars and clubs

Port Antonio *p50*
Roof Club, 11 West St. Disco and night spot where everything happens, with sign outside saying 'no drugs, no firecrackers, don't destroy furniture'. Popular with all types, melting pot of excitement, loud, advisable for women to be escorted or in a group, weekends best nights. For other suggestions, see the Nightlife page on http://myportantonio.com.

The north coast

The north coast attracts the majority of visitors to Jamaica, with thousands arriving by cruise ship in Ocho Rios and thousands more staying in all-inclusive resorts along the coast, principally at Montego Bay, the site of the international airport. There are well-known attractions such as Dunn's River Falls, but also less infamous places to visit away from the crowds: the fine Georgian town of Falmouth, now hosting cruise ships, caves in the Cockpit Country, or the Rocklands Feeding Station, a delightful garden where the doctor hummingbird is tame enough to drink sugar syrup from a bottle in your hand. Montego Bay is brash and fun-loving, attracting the party crowd, but away from the hip strip there are some architectural and anthropological sights worth exploring.

Kingston to Port Maria → *For listings, see pages 67-73.*

The Kingston to Port Maria road (the Junction Road) takes about two hours and there are plenty of minibuses. It passes through **Castleton Botanical Gardens** ① *T927 1257, www.jnht.com, open from 0530, closes 1800 Oct-Feb, 1830 Mar-Sep,* in a very tranquil setting and well worth a visit. Dating from 1862, the gardens became one of the finest in the world, stocked with over 4000 species of plants from Kew Gardens in London. In 1897 there were 180 different palms growing there and the gardens are still lush with flowering and medicinal plants. The road divides the gardens, but you can visit either side, take a picnic, swim in the Wag Water River or just enjoy the shade and listen to the birds.

Port Maria to Oracabessa → *For listings, see pages 67-73.*

Port Maria

Port Maria itself is a sleepy and decaying old banana port not without charm and with lots of goats. The Courthouse, although a replica after the 1821 building was gutted by fire in 1988 and reopened as a Civic Centre in 2000, was the scene of some crucial political trials. Perhaps the most famous was that of Alexander Bustamante in 1942, who was charged with manslaughter. Clearly a political trial, as he had only just been released from detention, he was supported by the workers whom he had championed in the 1938 labour struggles. Nevertheless, it was only after the intervention of his cousin and political rival, Norman Manley, who brought his legal skills to his defence after the trial appeared to be going against him, that Bustamante was acquitted. Both men are now National Heroes.

Brimmer Hall Great House

ⓘ *T974 2244, Mon-Fri 0900-1600.*

Southwest of Port Maria is this house, a single-storey, airy and spacious 18th-century plantation house with high ceilings and wide veranda. The furniture is all antique and the rooms are beautifully laid out, while the stables outside have been converted to shops, although they are rather run down. You get a tour of the house and a jitney ride around the working plantation to see how the crops are grown and then to sample them. On cruise ship itineraries, so it can get crowded.

Firefly

ⓘ *www.firefly-jamaica.com, 0800-1800, US$10, 20-min tour of house and garden.*

A few kilometres northwest of PM is Noel Coward's Jamaican home. Although now owned by Chris Blackwell's Island Outpost, much of the contents belong to the **Jamaica National Heritage Trust**. Time and the elements have not been kind to the property and it is currently under review by the Noël Coward Estate, the Blackwell family and the Jamaican government to save it for the future. In the meantime it is open to the public, is on the cruise ship itineraries and can be hired for weddings and other functions. It is evocative of a stylish era and a highlight if you are interested in the theatre or film stars of that period, plus the view is magnificent. Noel Coward's other property, **Blue Harbour**, is about 1 km away; this was his first home, where he used to entertain film stars, royalty etc, but he became tired of the crowds and built Firefly on the hill above as a one-bedroom retreat so he could not have guests. Coward died at Firefly in 1973 and is buried in the garden. Blue Harbour is now a guesthouse (see Where to stay, page 67).

Oracabessa

Oracabessa is another old banana port but with a fascinating political, social and artistic history. Named Oro Cabeza, or golden head, by the Spanish, it was later developed as a plantation economy by the British. In 1834, the Rev James Phillippo arrived in the community and upset the political order. He was a pioneer of Free Villages and joined forces with the Maroons to force the local landowner to sell land so that free slaves could build houses, schools and community buildings as well as farm their own land. Phillippo bought the land and sold it to the people on the understanding that they would pay him back as and when they could afford to. Within three years they owned the land outright and became the model for other Free Villages to follow. Their economic success, while initially strong, was set back by hurricanes and floods at the end of the 19th century and Oracabessa went into decline.

It was saved by an American woman, Ruth Owen, who was married to a British officer posted to Jamaica. She had read about Phillippo's work and wanted to build on it. Her husband built roads and schools, while she encouraged local people to develop skills as artists and craftspeople, selling their work in the USA. She also built a lovely house, **Golden Clouds**, which still stands today, where she entertained international celebrities and returned each winter even after the couple had moved abroad.

In 1946 Oracabessa welcomed its next famous visitor to become a resident. **Ian Fleming** wrote all the James Bond books at his house, **Golden Eye**, where he entertained the rich and famous. In 1976, 12 years after Fleming's death, the house was bought by Bob Marley, who then sold it to Chris Blackwell. His company, **Island Outpost**, www.islandoutpost.com, then bought more land in the 1990s and created a major tourist attraction with villas for rent. The James Bond Beach Club is in front of the house, the beach is small but highly recommended, as safe and child-friendly, with a bar and restaurant and watersports.

Artists and musicians continue to frequent Golden Eye; concerts are held on the lawns and those performing at James Bond Beach have included Rihanna and Ziggy Marley.

UB40 have a recording studio in Oracabessa, the town has been used for many film locations and the area is known as an artists' community with several studios and galleries. In 2010 the **Oracabessa Fish Sanctuary** was established to protect marine life offshore up to the edge of the Cayman Trough.

Boscobel

To the west of Oracabessa is Boscobel, home of the new Ian Fleming International Airport, designed to receive flights for Ocho Rios but currently dealing mainly with private flights.

Kingston to Ocho Rios → *For listings, see pages 67-73.*

The journey from Kingston to Ocho Rios follows a spectacular route, up the gorge of the **Rio Cobre**, then across Mount Diablo. **Faith's Pen**, right on the top, is an enormous collection of huts selling food and drink, mostly jerk chicken, pork or fish, festival, boiled or roasted corn, soup and natural juices or sodas, and great for a stop. The last section of road whizzes round a series of blind corners as you go through **Fern Gully**, a marvel of unspoilt tropical vegetation. Driving time is one hour 50 minutes by bus.

Ocho Rios → *For listings, see pages 67-73.*

Ocho Rios stands on a bay sheltered by reefs and surrounded by coconut groves, sugar cane and fruit plantations. The town has become very popular, with many cruise ships making a stop here. It is 103 km east of Montego Bay and claims some of the best beaches on the island. The beach in town, safe and well organized with facilities, is 200 m from Main Street where most of the shops and vehicle hire companies can be found. A landscaped and paved boardwalk, the 'One Love Trail', leads from Ocho Rios and Island Village shopping and entertainment complex adjacent to the cruise ship pier (food, music, cinema, art, beach, casino and gaming) to the surrounding attractions of Dunn's River Falls and Dolphin Cove. Recommended are the **Shaw Park Gardens** ① *T974 2723, daily 0800-1700. US$20 including tour*, an easy walk from the town centre, up the hill on the edge of town. Built on several tiers, different plants grow on each altitude and there are lovely views down over the town. An added feature is the waterfall in the gardens, a pleasant place to come and spend some time with a picnic and a swimsuit.

The scenery around the town is an attraction in itself. Most spectacular are the beauty spots of **Roaring River Falls**, and **Dunn's River Falls** ① *T974 4767, www.dunnsriverfallsja. com, daily 0830-1600 or from 0700 for cruise ships, US$20, 4-10s US$12, locker US$5 plus refundable security fee of US$3, water shoes US$7 (rental) or US$17 (purchase) but not necessary if you move with care*, tumbling into the Caribbean with invigorating salt- and freshwater bathing at its foot. It takes anything up to an hour to climb the falls, depending on how many people there are. Get there early before the coach parties arrive, Friday is the least crowded day; it's a five-minute bus ride (US$1) from Ocho Rios, or one-hour drive from Montego Bay (beware of pseudo guides who hang around and take you somewhere totally different, then try to sell you marijuana). The falls on Roaring River are less than 1 km west, by the hydroelectric station; they are less crowded but also less dramatic.

Opposite the entrance to Dunn's River Falls is **Dolphin Cove** ① *T974 5335, www.dolphincoveja.com, 0830-1730*, a large dolphinarium where captive dolphins and sharks are taught tricks for the entertainment of tourists like in a circus. As with any wild animal kept in captivity, think carefully before interacting with them. Accidents have happened and the animals can turn nasty.

Harmony Hall art gallery ① *T975 4222, www.harmonyhall.com, Tue-Sun 1000-1730*, just east of Ocho Rios, is worth a visit. There are frequent exhibitions of paintings and sculpture in a classic gingerbread house, as well as crafts, clothes and other gifts to buy. There is also a very good Italian restaurant downstairs, **Toscanini's** ① *T975 4785, Tue-Sun 1200-1415, 1900-2215*. The house itself is a National Monument and a fine example of Jamaican-Georgian architecture, typical of plantation houses of the late 19th century with its balustrades and gingerbread fretwork. If you have your own transport you could combine a visit to Harmony Hall with some time on **Reggae Beach**, 2 km east of White River Bridge in a little cove between Little Bay and Frankfort Bay. A bright sign on the seaward side of the main road marks a somewhat inconspicuous entrance leading to a long, shaded driveway and then a beach hideaway bustling with activity. It is an easy going spot with clean water and a nice beach, but you also get jerk chicken, roasts at festivals, reggae music, dominoes and Red Stripe beer to complete the picture.

Ocho Rios to Falmouth → *For listings, see pages 67-73.*

Sevilla Nueva

Sevilla Nueva, some 14.5 km to the west of Ocho Rios, is the place where the Spanish first settled in 1509. Spanish settlers built a sugar factory here but the swamps, mosquitoes and fevers forced them to relocate, founding Spanish Town in 1538. The ruins of the fort still remain and the post-1655 British sugar plantation known as New Seville. The Great House and property is now called the **Seville Great House and Heritage Park** ① *T972 9407, daily 0900-1700, last tour 1600, US$15, children US$6*, managed by the **Jamaica National Heritage Trust** as a museum. The house dates from 1745, when it was a two-storey building, but the top floor blew off in a hurricane in 1898 and was never replaced. In the grounds overlooking the ocean are the remains of a water wheel used to power the sugar mill, the overseer's house and a barbecue pit used for roasting allspice grown on the plantation. Guided tours are professional and informative and give you a good understanding of the island's heritage. It is considered one of the country's most important cultural heritage sites and is on the tentative list for a UNESCO World Heritage Site. There have been people living here since prehistoric times and there are archaeological remains dating back to AD 600, including the Taíno village of Maima.

Offshore, marine archaeologists are investigating the **St Ann's Bay** area for sunken ships. Salvaged timbers are believed to have come from two disabled caravels, the *Capitana* and the *Santiago de Palos*, abandoned at Sevilla Nueva probably in 1503 during Columbus' last visit to Jamaica. **Mammee Beach** is beautiful and is much less crowded than Ocho Rios, though there is no shade.

Runaway Bay and around

Continuing west along the coast is **Runaway Bay**, an attractive and friendly resort with lots of hotels. There is a good reef offshore, popular with divers and snorkelers and a couple of wrecked aircraft underwater, a dive site now called Ganja Planes, for obvious reasons. Runaway Bay is named for the Spanish governor Ysasi, who left quickly for Cuba in a canoe when he saw the English coming.

The people and their religions

Jamaica is a fascinating blend of cultures from colonial Britain, African slavery and immigrants from China, India and the Middle East. Reggae and Rastafariansim have become synonymous with Jamaica, and Bob Marley and Peter Tosh are just two of the greats to have been born here. Over 90% of Jamaicans are of West African descent. Because of this, Ashanti words still figure very largely in the local dialect (patois). There are also Chinese, East Indians and Christian Arabs as well as those of British descent and other European minorities. There is considerable poverty on the island, which has created social problems and some tension, although Jamaicans are naturally friendly, easy-going and international in their outlook (more people of Jamaican origin live outside Jamaica than inside).

The predominant religion is Protestantism, but there is also a Roman Catholic community, as well as followers of the Church of God, Baptists, Anglicans, Seventh Day Adventists, Pentecostals, Methodists and others. The Jewish, Moslem, Hindu and Bahai religions are also practised. Jamaicans are a very religious people and it is said that Jamaica has more churches per square mile than anywhere else in the world. To a small degree, early adaptations of the Christian faith, Revival and Pocomania, survive, but the most obvious local minority sect is Rastafarianism (see box, page 28).

The **Green Grotto Caves** ① *T973 2841, www.greengrottocavesja.com, US$20, children US$10, 0900-1600, 45-min tour,* formerly known as the Runaway Bay Caves, were once a haven for runaway slaves and smugglers, a labyrinthine limestone cave with stalagmites and stalagtites extending for 1525 m with chambers, light holes and a subterranean lake. Tours are of two caves, Runaway and Green Grotto.

Only 8 km away from Runaway Bay is **Discovery Bay** where Columbus possibly made his first landing. The **Columbus Park**, an outdoor museum, has exhibits and relics of various periods of Jamaican history. The land was donated by the Kaiser Bauxite Company, whose bauxite shipping terminal is rather a blot on the landscape. Columbus called the bay Puerto Seco, dry port, because of its lack of water. The beach, which is open to the public, still bears that name.

Nine Mile

If you turn inland from Runaway Bay, through the country town of Brown's Town, the B3 road will bring you to Alexandria and thence to the village of Nine Mile, where Bob Marley was born and spent his childhood. His body was brought here after his death and now lies in the Bob Marley Mausoleum with his guitar inside a small church. His mother and half-brother are also buried here, as are his grandparents. Fans come at any time of year to pay their respects, but crowds come here in February to celebrate his birthday, with his music being played all night. There are many guides and souvenir sellers outside, but inside the compound there are genuine Rastafari guides. Everywhere is painted green, red and yellow, the Rastafari colours symbolizing nature, blood and sunshine. Expect considerable hassling and everyone will want a tip, the guide, the musicians, everyone. Tour parties are hurried through, ready for the next group. This is a commercial venture.

Falmouth and around → *For listings, see pages 67-73.*

Falmouth is a charming small town about 32 km east of Montego Bay. It is the best example of a Georgian town and the **Jamaica National Heritage Trust** has declared the whole town a National Monument. It has a fine colonial courthouse, a church, some 18th-century houses with wrought-iron balconies, and **Antonio's**, a famous place to buy beach shirts. Much of the town centre has been pedestrianized, including Water Square. Sugar, molasses and rum were exported from Falmouth, but its waterfront is now dominated by a new cruise ship port big enough to receive the huge Oasis class ships. Carrying the Georgian theme further, the port area has been designed as a model 18th century town with cobbled streets, shops, restaurants, bars and parks. Trams cars and horse-drawn carriages take visitors on tours around town.

A popular excursion from Falmouth is to go rafting from **Martha Brae** village inland from Falmouth ① *T952 0889, www.jamaicarafting.com, 0900-1600. US$65 on 2-person raft although package tours are available which include transport, drinks, snacks, etc.* Expert rafters guide the 9-m craft very gently for the one-hour trip to the coast. The bamboo rafts are hand built by the captains and are used for four months before they have to be replaced. It is a beautiful, shady river with a colourful legend of a Taíno witch. She was thought to have lured Spanish gold hunters to a cave in search of treasure, never to be seen again. To get there, take a local bus from Montego Bay to Falmouth, hitchhike or walk 9.5 km to upper station; end station is about 5 km from Falmouth. Also operated by River Raft Ltd in the same area is **Jamaica Swamp Safari Village** ① *Foreshore Rd, T952 0889, US$15, children US$8, bar, restaurant*, a crocodile farm and small zoo where you can see lazy crocodiles with equally laid-back guides. In 1972 the crocodiles were used in the Bond movie, Live and Let Die, with the owner, Ross Kananga, standing in for Roger Moore in the scene where he escapes by running across the backs of the crocodiles. The producers were so impressed that they gave the name Kananga to the villain in the film.

Some 10 miles inland, the 18th-century plantation Great House of **Good Hope** ① *T469 3444, www.goodhopejamaica.com, horse riding daily 0800-1630, US$35 for 1½ hrs*, set in beautiful park land, has wonderful views over Martha Brae River, the Queen of Spain valley and the Cockpit Mountains. Nowadays it offers deluxe accommodation, as well as day tours around the house and grounds, with its old water wheel, kiln and other bits of the old sugar mill, good birdwatching and horse riding – some of the best trail riding in Jamaica.

An exciting attraction, 2.5 km east of Falmouth, is a bioluminescent lagoon, known locally as the **Luminous Lagoon**, although officially it is called Oyster Bay, where the water comes alive at night with sparkling blue-green lights from marine micro-organisms called dinoflagellates. The lagoon is said to be the most active bioluminescent lake in the world. A dark, moonless night, a local guide with typical Jamaican sense of humour, and a small power launch, are all that you need. Go as late as possible for maximum darkness and if there has been no rain for a couple of days it will be even better. The **Glistening Waters Restaurant & Marina** offers regular boat tours after dark taking up to 30 passengers, US$25 (see page 70), but you can negotiate with local boatmen to take you out and go swimming in the lagoon. Less than five minutes out, the pitch-black water behind the boat begins to illuminate, leaving a blue-green-white trail in its wake. When the boat stops, streaks of light flash intermittently in every direction, caused by small fry jumping out of the water. Larger fish tunnelling through the water carry a wake of luminescence with them. Collect some of the water in your hand and shake it to see it sparkle for several seconds.

The Maroons

When Columbus landed on Jamaica in 1494 it was inhabited by peaceful Taíno Indians living in over 200 villages, most of them on the south coast, especially around what is now Old Harbour. Under Spanish occupation, which began in 1509, the race faced harsh slavery and virtual extinction. Most died but some escaped into the mountains. Gradually African slaves were brought in to provide the labour force. In 1655 an English expeditionary force landed at Passage Fort and met with little resistance other than that offered by a small group of Spanish settlers and a larger number of African slaves who took refuge in the mountains, co-existing with the remaining Taínos. The Spaniards abandoned the island after about five years, but the slaves and their descendants, who became known as Maroons, waged war against the new colonists for 80 years until the 1730s although there was another brief rebellion in 1795. Some of their descendants still live in the Cockpit Country, where the Leeward Maroons hid, and around Nanny Town where the Windward Maroons hid.

Cockpit Country → For listings, see pages 67-73.

ⓘ *For tours in the Cockpit Country call the Southern Trelawny Environmental Agency, T610 0818, www.stea.net, also on Facebook. Various tours available, the Quashi tour US$70, Rocky Fort Cockpit Trek US$55, Paradise picnic US$55, Bunthill nature walk US$55 and Cockpit Country Underground Adventure US$60. Kenneth Watson is a tour guide, T952 4546.*

This is a strange and virtually uninhabited area to the south of Falmouth. It consists of a seemingly endless succession of high bumps made of limestone rock. The tourist office and some hotels in Montego Bay organize day trips to **Maroon Town** and **Accompong**, the headquarters of the Maroons who live in the Cockpit Country area. An annual festival, the **Annual Accompong Maroon Festival**, is held here on 4-6 January with traditional music and dance, to commemorate the treaty with the British giving the Maroons lands and autonomy. Older locals can accurately describe what happened at the last battle between the Maroons and the British forces.

Places in Cockpit Country

Ask to see the **Wondrous Caves** at Elderslie near Accompong. If you have a car take the road on the east side of the Cockpit Country from Duncans (near Falmouth) to Clark's Town. From there the road deteriorates to a track, impassable after a few kilometres even for 4WD vehicles, to **Barbecue Bottom** and on to Albert Town. The views from Barbecue Bottom are truly spectacular (the track is high above the Bottom) and this is wonderful birding country. If you wish to walk in the Cockpit Country make your way (no public transport) to the **Windsor Caves** due south of Falmouth. They are full of bats which make a spectacular mass exit at dusk. There are local guides. The underground rivers in the caves run for miles, but are only for the experienced and properly equipped potholer. A locally published book called *Jamaica Underground* details the many caves and good walks in the area. It is possible to walk from the Windsor Caves across the middle of the Cockpit Country to Troy on the south side (about eight hours). It is essential to have a local guide and to make a preliminary trip to the Windsor Caves to engage him. Make sure that he really does know the way because these days this crossing is very rarely made even by the locals. It is also vastly preferable to be met with transport at Troy because you will still be in a pretty remote area.

Montego Bay → *For listings, see pages 67-73.*

About 193 km from Kingston, on the island's northwest coast, Montego Bay is Jamaica's principal tourist centre with all possible watersports amenities. Known familiarly as Mo' Bay, it has superb natural features, sunshine most of the year round, a beautiful coastline with miles of white sand, deep blue water never too cold for bathing and gentle winds that make sailing a favourite sport. **Doctor's Cave** is the social centre of beach life, while **Gloucester Avenue** is one of the busiest streets for tourists, lined with duty-free shops, souvenir arcades, hotels and restaurants.

Arriving in Montego Bay

The **Donald Sangster International Airport** is only 3 km from the town centre, 10-20 minutes, shared van or bus US$10 per person, private taxi or van US$30-55. Most hotels organize transfers for their guests, check with the transportation desks after you've been through Customs if you have booked this service. The **tourist office** ① *T952 4425*, is on Cornwall Beach, Gloucester Avenue. *▸▸ See also Transport, page 73, for further details.*

Places in Montego Bay

Of interest to the sightseer are the remaining battery, cannons and powder magazine of an old British fort, **Fort Montego**, with landscaped gardens and crafts market (free), and the 18th-century church of **St James** in Montego Bay, built in 1778 and restored after earthquake damage. There are a few Georgian buildings, such as the **Town House Restaurant** ① *16 Church St* (local art gallery next door), and the Georgian Court at the corner of Union and Orange streets. The centre of town is **Sam Sharpe Square**, named after the slave who led a rebellion in 1831-1832, now a National Hero. Sam 'Daddy' Sharpe was hanged here on 23 May 1832 and the British killed about 500 of his followers. In one corner of the square is the Cage, a tiny prison built in 1806 to detain escaped slaves or drunken sailors. Next to it is the Ring, an amphitheatre where slave auctions were held and later cockfights. The Burchell Memorial Church, established by the Baptist missionary, Thomas Burchell, was where Samuel Sharpe served as a deacon. The **Museum of St James** ① *Civic Centre, T971 9417, Tue-Fri 0900-1700, Sat 1000-1500, Sun 1200-1700, US$3, children US$1*, displays the history of the parish from pre-Columbian times to the present in the restored Old Courthouse on Sam Sharpe Square.

    Montego Bay Freeport is the cruise ship port and also the Montego Bay Yacht Club, on an outcrop on the west side of the bay. Regattas are held here and you can charter a yacht or a sport fishing boat for a half or full day. The **Montego Bay Marine Park** (www.mbmp.org) extends from the high tide mark to a depth of 100 m over the whole of the bay, including two fish sanctuaries where fishing is prohibited. This amounts to 15.3 sq km of reef, sea grass and mangrove swamps from Rum Bottle Bay in the west to Tropical Beach by the airport in the east.

Beaches

Gloucester Av is known as the 'Hip Strip', for the beaches, bars and nightlife. The beaches along here are private and you will have to pay to enter, but this will entitle you to clean sand and changing facilities. **Doctor's Cave Beach** ① *Gloucester Av, daily 0830-1730, US$5,*

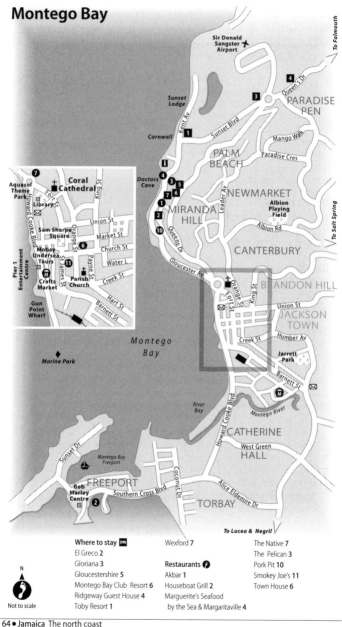

Montego Bay

Sir Donald
Sangster
Airport

To Falmouth

Sunset
Lodge

Kent Av

Sunset Blvd

4 Queen's Dr

3

PARADISE
PEN

Cornwall

1

Mango Walk

Paradise Cres

PALM
BEACH

Coral
Cathedral

7

Aquasol
Theme
Park

Library

Torr

St Gun

Doctors
Cave

1

4

3 **5**

7 **6**

1

2

10

Leader Av

NEWMARKET

Albion
Playing
Field

Albion Rd

To Salt Spring

MIRANDA
HILL

CANTERBURY

Howard Cooke Blvd

Union St

Sam Sharpe
Square

Orange St

Market St

Church St

6

Queens Dr

Gloucester Av

BRANDON HILL

Pier 1
Entertainment
Centre

Mobay
Undersea
Tours

St James St

Payne St

Water L

11

Crafts
Market

Parish
Church

Creek St

Fort St

Orange St

St Gun

Union St

JACKSON
TOWN

Gun
Point
Wharf

Hart St

Barnett St

Creek St

Humber Av

Jarrett
Park

Montego
Bay

Barnett St

Marine Park

Montego River

River
Bay

Howard Cooke Blvd

CATHERINE
HALL

West Green

Sunset Dr

Montego Bay
Freeport

FREEPORT

Bob
Marley
Centre

2

Southern Cross Blvd

Coconut Dr

Alice Eldemire Dr

TORBAY

To Lucea & Negril

N

Not to scale

Where to stay 🛏
El Greco **2**
Gloriana **3**
Gloucestershire **5**
Montego Bay Club Resort **6**
Ridgeway Guest House **4**
Toby Resort **1**

Wexford **7**

Restaurants 🍴
Akbar **1**
Houseboat Grill **2**
Marguerite's Seafood
  by the Sea & Margaritaville **4**

The Native **7**
The Pelican **3**
Pork Pit **10**
Smokey Joe's **11**
Town House **6**

under 12s half price, has underwater coral gardens, so clear that they can be seen without effort from glass-bottomed boats. It is relaxed and you can sunbathe quietly although sometimes it can get crowded with cruise ship passengers. This is the best beach in Montego Bay, only 300 m long but kept clean and tidy. There are water toys, restaurants and bars. You are not allowed to bring in food and drink. Chairs, umbrellas and snorkel gear are available for rent. **Cornwall Beach** ⓘ *Gloucester Av, lifeguards daily 0900-1700, US$5 entry, or US$12 entry with sunbed and umbrella*, is often closed for the exclusive use of cruise ship passengers but is also popular with locals on Sundays when they hold beach parties. It is not very big and can be crowded, but it has a floating trampoline, an inflatable iceberg, beach volleyball court and very clean showers and toilets. The **Walter Fletcher** beach has been converted to the **Aquasol Beach Park** ⓘ *Gloucester Av, T979 9447, daily 0900-1700, US$5, beach chair rental US$4*, a watersports theme park with water slides, US$1 for 10 minutes. This is probably the least attractive of the beaches, with loud music and older facilities. Scuba diving can be arranged through about a dozen operators, several of which have outlets at more than one hotel.

Around Montego Bay

If doing any excursions around Montego Bay you are likely to find parties of cruise ship passengers joining you so it is often a good idea to time your visits when places are less crowded. **Rose Hall Great House** ⓘ *T953 2323, www.rosehall.com, daily 0915-1715, US$20, children US$10*, is the grandest of all Jamaica's plantation houses, set high on a hill overlooking the coast. Building started in 1750 by George Ash, who named it after his wife, Rose, but it wasn't finished until 1780 when it was owned by John Palmer, Rose's fourth husband. It is a calendar house, with 365 windows, 52 doors and 12 bedrooms. A lively legend of witchcraft surrounds Annie Palmer, the wife of one of their descendants. She too had three husbands and several lovers who, it is claimed, she murdered before dying herself in mysterious circumstances, probably insane, and subsequently haunting the house. She was buried nearby so that her spirit could be reunited with her body. It is now believed that her symptoms were evidence of lead poisoning through eating her meals off lead plates, which could also have accounted for the death of her menfolk. After emancipation the house fell into disrepair and then ruin. However, in 1965 the Rollins family bought it and started renovations, keeping as true as possible to the original, both in building materials and furnishings.

    Greenwood Great House ⓘ *T953 1077, www.greenwoodgreathouse.com, daily 0900-1800, US$20 including tour*, 24 km east of Montego Bay, 11 km west of Falmouth, was built in 1780-1800 by the forefathers of the poet Elizabeth Barrett Browning. It has a colourful avenue of bougainvillea and mimosa and a panoramic view over the coast from the veranda which is really spectacular. It is another picturesque Great House, often used for weddings or photo shoots, with antique furniture and a rare collection of musical instruments and books. Unusually, the current owners actually live in the house and sleep in the antique beds. The first Barrett family member came over with the British expeditionary force which captured the island from the Spanish. He was granted land on Jamaica and his fortunes prospered. By the middle of the 18th century his descendents had amassed a huge estate of over 84,000 acres and 2000 slaves as well as a house in London. Elizabeth Barrett Browning's father Edward returned to England with his brother and sister and an annual income of £60,000, a fortune at the time. He left his cousin, Richard, in charge of the estate in Jamaica and he became a pillar of the powerful elite, including Speaker of the House of Assembly. Elizabeth never set foot in Jamaica but lived off the family wealth.

South of Montego Bay is the **Barnett Estate & Bellefield Great House** ① *Granville, T952 2382, www.bellefieldgreathouse.com, tours 0900-1600, 2-3 hrs, US$28 or US$40 with lunch, US$52 with Appleton rum tasting*, which can also date its founding back to 1655 and the arrival of the conquering British. Nicholas Jarrett was the first of the family on the island and built up influence and political power as well as land. The Kerr Jarrett family owned most of the land on which Montego Bay now stands, including the Barnett Estate with its magnificent 18th century Great House. You can tour the working plantation in a jitney and then visit the house before having lunch under the old guango tree, serenaded by mento music.

Southwest of Montego Bay is the unmissable **Rocklands Bird Sanctuary** at **Anchovy** ① *T952 2009, daily 1230-1730; no children under 5, US$20, children US$5*, where the doctor bird humming birds hover to eat sugar syrup from a little bottle and will even perch on your finger. There are lots of other birds too, all very tame, and Fritz, the caretaker, will take you on a walk around the property to see todies and other birds if you are interested. The sanctuary was started by Lisa Salmon in the late 1950s, who began to feed the hummingbirds in her garden. After her death, Fritz continued her work and is extremely knowledgeable. The road to Anchovy is very rough. Five kilometres west of Anchovy is **Lethe**, the starting point for rafting down the Great River. Some 16 km from Montego Bay on the Savanna-La-Mar road is the **Montpelier Great House**, on the site of the old Montpelier sugar factory, destroyed during the 1831 rebellion. South of Anchovy, about 40 km from Montego Bay, is **Seaford Town**, which was settled by Germans in the 1830s. About 200 of their descendants survive.

Continuing along the island's west end, the road passes through **Green Island** (before reaching Negril). Green Island, 46 km from Lucea, is a lovely spot with several pretty fishing villages, such as Cousins Cove, and small guesthouses and seaside cottages for rent.

The north coast listings

For hotel and restaurant price codes and other relevant information, see pages 12-14.

🛏 Where to stay

Port Maria to Oracabessa *p55*

$$$$ Blue Harbour Villas, northwest of Port Maria, T725 0289, www.blueharb.com. 3 villas on property which once belonged to Noel Coward. You can book room only, full board (meals use local produce, mostly organic, vegetarian available), or you can reserve the whole resort. Accommodation for 2-20 guests in the **Villa Grande** (2 bedrooms), the **Villa Chica** (1 bedroom) and the **Villa Rose** (3-4 bedrooms), all much as Coward left it, including his library. Saltwater pool, coral beach, kayaking, snorkelling, gardens, lovely views.

$$$$ Goldeneye, Oracabessa, T622 9007, www.goldeneye.com. A member of the Island Outpost group, this luxurious, secluded resort has been developed by Chris Blackwell at the home of James Bond author, Ian Fleming (see above). 1- and 2-bedroom villas have either a beachfront or a lagoon setting, while cottages with their own deck and kayak stand on the lagoon. There is also the top-of-the-range Fleming Villa. Contemporary decorations and amenities, **Bizot Bar** serves breakfast and lunch, the **Gazebo Restaurant and Lounge** has Jamaican and international cuisine. Plenty of fitness and other activities, excursions and spa.

$$$$-$$ Strawberry Fields Together!, Robin's Bay, 3 km from village, T655 0136/999 7169, www.strawberryfieldstogether.com. Standard cottages for 2-6 people and luxury cottages (sleep 2-4), all with private bath, some with kitchen, tent sites (US$15) and tent rental, transport essential or arrange pick-up with resort, meal plans, adventure and ecotour packages available, restaurant, nature trails, trampoline, volleyball, ping pong. Good for

family or special interest groups, Jamaican family fun days at weekends with barbeque, music and singing.

$$$ Casa Maria, Castle Gardens, Port Maria, T725 0157, www.casamariahotel.net. 20 rooms, beach, pool, restaurants, bars. Relaxing, private, also used for weddings, seminars and parties.

Ocho Rios *p57*

The coast is dominated by many huge, all-inclusive resorts, usually booked from abroad.

$$$$ Jamaica Inn, T974 2514, www.jamaicainn.com. Award-winning hotel, top of its league since it opened in 1950, casually elegant but unpretentious. 48 spacious and comfortable suites and cottages, all with balconies, meal plans available, gourmet dining, room service, pool, private beach, KiYara Ocean Spa, facilities for the disabled, Winston Churchill used to stay here and Noel Coward drank here.

$$$$-$$$ The Blue House, T994 1367, www.thebluehousejamaica.com. Bed-and-breakfast villa 2 miles east of Ocho Rios, 4 luxurious rooms and a cottage, tasteful decorations, good facilities, as well as Jamaican breakfast, lunch and dinner are available, served communally. Swimming pool, beach shuttles, offers short-term retreats, Christian missions and volunteer opportunities and weddings and honeymoon packages.

$$$$-$$$ Hibiscus Lodge, 83 Main St, T974 2676, www.hibiscusjamaica.com. 26 rooms in gardens overlooking sea, room rates according to ocean, pool or garden view, pool, spa services, tennis, **Almond Tree** restaurant and **Swinging** bar. Within walking distance of town.

$$$$-$$$ Mystic Ridge Resort, 17 DaCosta Dr, T974 9831, www.mysticridgejamaica.com. Bright, cheerful suites, standard rooms and apartments in pleasant gardens on a Bluff, overlooking Ocho Rios. Rooms and suites are in blocks, private balconies, swimming pool, tennis courts, beach shuttle, June Plum restaurant and bar, Samambaia Spa. In same group as **Mystic Mountain Rainforest Adventures**, www.rainforestadventure.com, to which guests have a discount.

$$$-$$ Little Shaw Park Guest House, 21 Shaw Park Rd, Milford, T974 2177, www.littleshawparkguesthouse.com. Family-run, studio apartments, some with kitchenette, and simple rooms, cheaper with fan than with a/c, with bath, Wi-Fi, gardens.

$$ La Penciano Guest House, 3 Short Lane, T974 5472. Rooms with shared or private bath, fan, TV, in centre and noisy, but clean and safe, friendly, bar (open Fri and Sat night) has views over Ocho Rios.

Ocho Rios to Falmouth p59

$$$ Cardiff Hotel and Spa, Runaway Bay, T973 6671, www.thecardiffhotel.com. Recently rebranded as an ecoresort, with suites and deluxe rooms, quiet, **Isabella's** restaurant with contemporary Jamaican cooking, access to private beach, shuttle to the golf club.

$$$ Piper's Cove Resort, Runaway Bay, T973 7156, www.piperscoveresortjamaica.com. Studio and 1-bedroom apartments with kitchenette, bathroom, balcony and all amenities. Meals are available but charged extra. With pool, gardens and beach, activities and excursions can be arranged.

Falmouth p61

$$$$ Silver Sands Villas and Beach Club, Silver Sands Estates, Duncan's, call **Jamaican Villa Vacations**, T954 2001 for bookings, www.silversands-jamaica.com. Private, comfortable villas, each with its own style, from 1- to 7-bedrooms available. Most have a/c rooms, TV, phone, private swimming pool, and friendly maid service (mainly for cooking). Easy access to the beach, snack shop, bar, games room, commissary and nightclub.

$$$ Fisherman's Inn, Rock, Falmouth, T954 3427, www.fishermansinnjamaica.com. On the main road, heading to St Ann, by the

Luminous Lagoon. 8 rooms and 2 suites built over the water, restaurant and bar where you can have an excellent seafood sunset dinner on the deck, the swimming pool is built on a jetty over the lagoon.

Montego Bay p63, map p64

There are some 60 all-inclusive resorts, hotels, guesthouses and villas listed by the tourist board and many more which are not.

$$$$-$$$ El Greco, 11 Queens Dr, T940 6116, www.elgrecojamaica.com. 93 deluxe, self-catering suites with balconies on hillside overlooking bay, also has Sea View Restaurant, direct elevator access to Gloucester Av and Doctor's Cave Beach, grocery store, Wi-Fi, pool, beach towels, tennis, laundry, tours offered.

$$$$-$$$ Gloucestershire, 92 Gloucester Av, T952 4420, www.thegloucestershire hotel.com. Cream and white building with blue awnings opposite Doctor's Cave Beach on the hip strip. Standard, deluxe a/c rooms and suites, with safe, TV and free Wi-Fi, most with balcony, pool, jacuzzi, gym, restaurant and café, breakfast included.

$$$$-$$$ Toby Resort, 1 Kent Av, T952 4370, www.tobyresorts.com. Rooms with pool or garden view, balcony, bath, simple, convenient for the 'Strip', swimming pool. Also has **Toby's Good Eats** for barbecued chicken and pork, other local and international dishes, meal plans available.

$$$$-$$$ Wexford, 39 Gloucester Av, T952 2854, www.thewexfordhotel.com. Across the road from the public beach, close to Margaritaville. Ocean view and deluxe rooms and suites, tiled floors, TV, a/c, balconies, **Rosella's** restaurant serves Caribbean cuisine.

$$$ Montego Bay Club Resort, Gloucester Av, T952 4310, lisafitz@epix.net, Montego-Bay-Club-Resort on Facebook. Dominant 12-storey apartment hotel with privately-owned studios and suites with kitchens and balconies in centre of tourist area overlooking Doctor's Cave Beach, pool, tennis, beauty salon, supermarket, maid service.

$$$-$$ Gloriana, 1-2 Sunset Blvd,
T979 0669, www.hotelgloriana.com.
Close to airport, 10 mins' walk from beach,
75 rooms and suites, TV, phone, some
with balcony, pool, bar, restaurant, garden,
entertainment at weekends, tours arranged.
$$$-$$ Ridgeway Guest House,
34 Queen's Dr, T952 2709, www.ridgeway
guesthouse.com. 5 mins' walk from airport,
free airport transfer, 10 rooms, bath, a/c
or fan, fruit trees in the garden for guests'
to help themselves, friendly, clean, family
atmosphere, run by brothers Christopher
and Colin Tatem.

Around Montego Bay *p65*
$$$$ Coyaba Beach Resort and Club,
Mahoe Bay, 8 km east of Montego Bay,
T953 9150, www.coyabaresortjamaica.com.
50 rooms and suites, 3 restaurants and bars,
gardens, pool, jacuzzi, private dock, tennis,
fitness room, hammocks on the shore,
family-owned.
$$$$ Half Moon, Rose Hall, a Rock Resort
at Rose Hall, on 160 ha adjoining beach,
T888-830 5974, www.halfmoon.rock
resorts.com. 197 luxury rooms and suites,
also Royal Villas with 5 to 7 bedrooms
with staff. There are 6 restaurants and
7 bars, spa, fitness centre, golf, tennis,
riding stables, childrens' activities and
unfortunately there's swimming with
dolphins in the resort's private lagoon.
$$$$ Round Hill Hotel and Villas, John
Pringle Dr, 10 mins west of Montego Bay
on 40-ha peninsula, T956 7050, www.round
hilljamaica.com. Originally a coconut and
pineapple plantation, it opened in the
1950s with the help of Noel Coward. It is
a hotel with oceanfront rooms, villa suites
and also has private villas which can be
rented. Celebrity villa owners include Paul
McCartney and Ralph Lauren. Meal plans
are available, **The Grill** restaurant, **Seaside
Terrace**, spa and fitness centre, infinity pool,
watersports, tennis and golf.
$$$$ The Tryall Club, Sandy Bay, Tryall,
T956 5660, www.tryallclub.com. On

a historic plantation, first sugar, then
coconuts, this 890-ha luxury villa complex
with a championship golf course is an elite
destination and National Heritage site with
a Georgian great house. As well as the golf
course it has its own beach, watersports,
tennis and nature programmes.
$$$ Royal Reef, 30 mins east of Mo'bay,
opposite turning for Greenwood, T953 1700,
www.royalreefja.com. 19 rooms, standard to
super deluxe, some with sea view, others look
on to road with patio, TV, a/c, bright white
tiled bathrooms, price negotiable in low
season, Jamaicans pay less than foreigners.
Cool lounge area with TV and games, piano,
restaurant, bar. Quiet area, go into Mo'bay
for nightlife. Salt and fresh water pools, man-
made sandy cove safe for kids, sea shallow
out to the reef, sea grass and mangroves.

🍴 Restaurants

Ocho Rios *p57*
On **Main St** there are restaurants offering
Jamaican, international or seafood cuisine.
$$$-$$ The Almond Tree, the restaurant at
the **Hibiscus Lodge**, T974 2813. See Where to
stay above. Jamaican food, nice atmsophere.
$$$ Café Aubergine, near Moneague, T973
0527. Wed-Sun 1200-2230. An upmarket
and tasteful restaurant in an 18th-century
house, European and Caribbean influences.
$$$-$$ Ocho Rios Village Jerk Centre,
DaCosta Dr, T974 2549. Open daily from
1000. Good value jerk chicken, pork, fish
and other local dishes.
$$ The Little Pub, 59 Main St, T795 1831.
Jamaican food and entertainment, also
serves breakfast.

Ocho Rios to Falmouth *p59*
$$ Scotchies Jerk Centre, Drax Hall at the
intersection of the St Ann's Bay to Ocho Rios
main road and Chalky Hill Rd, T794 9457. An
authentic Jamaican Jerk haunt (the original
branch is in Mo'Bay – see below – and there
is a branch in Kingston, too), popular, the
food and service are outstanding. Rustic but

nicely landscaped eating areas, absolutely delicious fish, pork and chicken meals.
$$ Ultimate Jerk Centre, Main St, Runaway Bay, T973 2054. Good, affordable food, with an oldies night on the last Sat of every month.

Falmouth p61
$$$ Glistening Waters Restaurant, Rock, T954 3229, www.glisteningwaters.com. Mon-Sat 0900-2130, Sun1200-2130, boat tours are nightly every 30 mins, 1900-2100. Restaurant specializes in fish and seafood. They also have a bar and a marina.

Montego Bay p63, map p64
Most restaurants are happy for guests to bring wine and will provide chillers and glasses. Rum is cheaper here than at airport duty-free shops. Service at restaurants can be begrudging but the food is excellent. On the way into town from the airport there are several reasonably priced restaurants.
$$$ Akbar, 71 Gloucester Av, T953 8240. At the **Half Moon** shopping village. Delicious, authentic Indian food.
$$$ Houseboat Grill, Southern Cross Blvd, Montego Freeport, T979 8845, www.the houseboatgrill.com. Open daily for dinner from 1800-2300. Bar opens at 1630. Lovely location, houseboat on the lagoon, pontoon ferry to board it, glass-bottom section fascinating for kids, lobster tank, tasty appetizers, vegetarian options, entrées mostly steak, lobster, fish and shrimp, international wine list. Move upstairs on deck for dessert and comfortable chairs to watch rays, tarpon and snook around the boat, romantic but insect repellent essential.
$$$ Ma Lou's, Coral Cliff Hotel and Entertainment Lounge, Gloucester Av. Gourmet restaurant owned by Miss Lou, a Jamaican of Chinese origin whose parents came from Bermuda and Isla Margarita, and her son Pepper. Culinary influences come from all round the islands. Lots of seafood, lobster and meat, wine from around the world, reservations essential, only seats

25 people in Jamaican-style chattel house, cheerful colours.
$$$ Marguerite's Seafood by the Sea, Gloucester Av, T952 4777, on the seafront. 2 restaurants, one posh with a/c and **Margaritaville** next door on a patio, T952 9609 (see Bars & clubs below). Sports bar and grill.
$$$ Town House, 16 Church St (see page 63), T952 2660. Open 1130-2300. The house is covered in bougainvillea overlooking Church Sq, dining on lower ground floor, very smart, dimmed lighting, linen napkins.
$$$-$$ The Native, 29 Gloucester Av, T979 2769. Open 0730-2230. Opposite **Aqua Sol**, upstairs to catch the breeze, very pleasant, lunch specials, local dishes, curried goat, brown stew pork, stewed peas, or try coconut crusted chicken with cinnamon banana, also salads, sandwiches, soups, seafood and vegetarian dishes. Parking.
$$$-$$ The Pelican, Gloucester Av, west of Coral Cliff, T952 3171, www.pelican grillja.com. Excellent breakfasts and dinners, good value, comfortable, popular, varied menu, vegetarian selection.
$$$-$$ Rum Jungle Café and Bar, Coral Cliff Hotel and Entertainment Lounge, Gloucester Av, T952 4130. Open 24 hrs. Tropical jungle decor, pirate climbing down a rope over the bar, lots of realistic plastic greenery. All-day breakfast American or Jamaican style, snacks such as potato skins, jerk fries, rotis, nachos, pizzas, vegetarian options, sandwiches, burgers, or main meals of ribs, steak and roasts. Great place to come for Sun brunch, 1000-1400, where you can try unusual Jamaican fruit, jackfruit, otaheite apple (purple skin, white flesh, pear-shaped) or star apple (purple and white). Plenty of rums to try and live entertainment.
$$ Baba Joe's, Kent Av, near airport on way to Whitehouse Village, just past **Sandals**, T979 1053. Excellent fish, local style.
$$ Pork Pit, 27 Gloucester Av, T940 3008, The-Pork-Pit on Facebook. Open 1100-2300 (till 2400 Fri-Sat). Jerk chicken, pork and ribs sold by weight, service basic.

$$ Scotchie's, Coral Gardens Villas, Rose Hall, near the **Holiday Inn**, T953 8041. Open 1100-2300. Just about as good as jerk gets; pork, chicken and fish available with just the right amount of spice, served wedded to roasted breadfruit, potato, yam or festival.
$$ Smokey Joe's, 19½ St James St, T940 3178. Open 0800-2200. Good local restaurant, also caterers.

🎵 Bars and clubs

Ocho Rios *p57*
Late night action usually takes place in the resorts and along James St also known as the reggae strip. Usually on Thu at 1900 the street comes alive with fire entertainers and booths offering local cuisine.
The Acropolis nightclub. Lively and fairly safe.
Amnesia Night Club, 70 Main St, T974-904 2633. Open Wed-Sun. Long-established Jamaican dancehall. There is an entry charge.
Jamaica'n Me Crazy, at the Sunset Jamaica Grande resort, www.sunsetjamaica grande.com. One of the top nightspots.
Strawberry's, 6 James Av, T898 1091. Sports bar, Jamaican restaurant and, at weekends, disco, popular with locals.

Montego Bay *p63, map p64*
Lots of hotels have discos and clubs. Apart from that, the 'Hip Strip', largely Gloucester Ave, is where most people go for shopping and entertainment. Harassment of tourists happens; exercise caution, especially at night.
Coral Cliff Entertainment Lounge, Gloucester Av, T952 4130. Open 24 hrs. Montego Bay has no casino, but here there are about 100 slot machines, big screen sports TV and live music or other shows on the stage. As well as **Ma Lou's** and the **Rum Jungle Café and Bar** (see above), it also has **Chillin'** bar and a boutique hotel.
Margaritaville Caribbean Bar and Grill, Gloucester Av, T952 4777, www.margarita villecaribbean.com. Now quite an institution, very popular with students if pricey,

52 flavours of Margaritas and 32-oz 'bong of beer', food available till 2200, sport on big TVs, Nintendo and kids' menu, waterslide from roof to sea, themed nights every day of the week, DJs, dancing. Daily from 1100, cover charge at Club Ville after US$10, except for `all-you-can-drink' parties on Wed and Fri, US$25. Next door and in the same group is **Blue Beat Ultra Lounge**, a jazz and martini club, with live music, Fri and Sat parties, meals and drinks. There are other branches of Margaritaville in Ocho Rios and Negril.
Pier One, on the waterfront, junction of Howard Cooke Blvd and Barnett St in River Bay, T952 2452, www.pieronejamaica.com. Look out for live concerts with well-known Jamaican reggae stars attracting an audience of up to 1000 people, loud and energetic, dancing, events through the week. Good food, everything from sandwiches to curry, eat indoors or outside, fast and friendly service, families welcome, big-screen TV for sports events. Bar serves variety of tropical drinks.

🛍 Shopping

Ocho Rios *p57*
Wassi Art, 16 Main St, T974 5044, www.wassiart.com. The pottery studio and showroom is delightful; there is a good selection and you can visit each artist. The clay is dug by hand from the Blue Mountains and transported in sacks on people's heads through the forest and across gullies.

⏰ What to do

Ocho Rios *p57*
Golf
Sandals Golf & Country Club, Upton, T975 0119/22. 18 holes, green fee US$100, golf free for **Sandals** guests. Caddies are mandatory and are not Sandals' employees, so tips as well as a fee are expected. Golf lessons, golf cart rentals, club rentals and shoe rental all available.

Horse riding

Polo is played on Sat afternoons at St Ann Polo Club, Drax Hall Estate, St Ann's Bay, near Ocho Rios, T376 1314, where there is a full equestrian centre including showjumping arena. Polo lessons can be arranged with Lesley-Anne Masterton Fong-Yee, a great international player and now a leading polo trainer in Jamaica. There is also polo at the **Polo and Equestrian Club of Oakbrook**, Shady Tree, T903 0224 for match details. International tournaments are held at **Chukka Cove Equestrian Centre**, Richmond Llandovery, St Ann's Bay, T972 2506.

Tour operators

Blue Mountain Bicycle Tours, Shop 15, Santa Maria Plaza, 121 Main St, T974 7075, www.bmtoursja.com. Tours include a 29-km downhill trip through the forest to a waterfall, but don't expect much from the bikes.
Chukka, T1-877-424 8552, www.chukka caribbean.com. A wide variety of adventure tours catering mainly to the cruise ship market: horse riding, zip-line, ATV safari, dune buggy, river tubing and whitewater rafting are all offered. Note, however, that horse riding in the sea, while many people's dream, is an ecological disaster. The horses' dung increases the level of nutrients in the sea, causing algae to grow on the coral and kill it.
Circle B, just southwest of St Ann's Bay, turn off at Priory, T913 4511, www.millertcs.com/circlebfarm, owned by former senator, Bob Miller. Very good tour of working plantation with a welcome drink and sample fruits of Jamaica; lunch can be included. There's also a hostel here with bunk bed accommodation and use of kitchen.
Mystic Mountain Rainforest Adventures, T866-759 8720, www.rainforestadventure. com. Jamaica Bobsled through the forest, Sky Explorer, Canopy Zipline, US$137.50 for combined package, but each can be purchased separately, also waterslide and pool, lookout tower, gardens and pavilion.
Prospect Plantation Tour, east of Ocho Rios, managed by Dolphin Cove, T994 1058, www.prospectplantationtour.com. Probably the most attractive and informative, and certainly the most accessible of the plantation tours, including lots of activities. Ride on an open jitney, ride horses, a segway or bike on scenic trails, take a camel safari or a Jamaican cooking lesson or feed the ostriches.

Ocho Rios to Falmouth *p59*

For diving and fishing, see box, page 75.

Golf

Runaway Bay Golf Club, www.jewelresorts. com/resorts/dunnsriver/activities/golf. 18 holes, free for guests at **Jewel Dunn's River Resort**.

Spectator sports

A magnificent multi-purpose stadium seating 25,000 was opened in 2007 at Greenfields, Trelawny, just east of Falmouth. Built with Chinese help for the Cricket World Cup, it hosted the opening ceremony and 4 warm-up matches beforehand. Sometimes used for football, the Reggae Boyz played a World Cup qualifier here in 2008 and some Caribbean Cup matches have been held here. It has also been used to stage the Jamaica Jazz & Blues Festival.

Cockpit Country *p62*
Tour operators

For caving, contact Mike Schwartz of **Windsor Great House**, T997 3832, windsor@cwjamaica.com, where there is rustic accommodation.
Sun Venture Tours (see page 43) offer tailor-made tours of the Cockpit Country Crossing (Troy to Windsor the preferred route, or for a less arduous hike, St Vincent to Clarks Town).

Montego Bay *p63, map p64*
Golf

Cinnamon Hill Golf Course, part of Hilton Rose Hall Resort & Spa, east of Montego Bay, T953 4772. 18 holes.

Half Moon Golf Club, T953 2560, www.half moon.rockresorts.com/activities/golf.asp. Advance booking necessary for this championship course, 18 holes, mandatory cart and caddy, also tennis and squash.
Ironshore Golf and Country Club, T953 3681, www.superclubs.com. A **SuperClubs** course, free for guests, 18 holes, green fee US$45.

Horse riding
Hotels can arrange riding with local stables and there are good facilities at the **Half Moon Equestrian Centre** at Half Moon Resort, T953 2286, www.horsebackriding jamaica.com. A beach ride of 1 hr 20 mins costs US$80. Dressage, jumping and polo lessons are also available for all levels.

⊖ Transport

Montego Bay *p63, map p64*
Air
Donald Sangster International Airport is a regional hub and there are good connections with lots of airlines landing here. Connections by air to Kingston and other Jamaican airports are limited. You can either take a charter plane, such as **TimAir**, www.timair.net, or **International Air Link**, www.intlairlink.net, or a helicopter shuttle, **Captain John's Island Hoppers**, www.jamaicahelicopterservices.com, or **Jamaica Customized Vacations & Services**, www.jcvtt.com.

Bus
The long-distance bus company, **Knutsford Express**, 10 Harbour Circle, near Pier 1, T971 1822, www.knutsfordexpress.com, runs from Montego Bay to **Falmouth**, **Ocho Rios**, **Kingston**, **Negril**, **Mandeville**, **Santa Cruz** and **Savanna la Mar**. The municipal bus system is called the **Montego Bay Metro**, T952 5500, and runs on 3 routes to the city centre, from Greenwood, from Sandy Bay and from Cambridge.

Route taxis run all over the place. Look for the red licence plate and a description of the route on the car door. They can get very full but go to outlying villages and towns where there is no other transport. You may need to change routes along the way and a great deal of patience is required.

Taxi
Private taxis can be found at hotels or flag one down in the street. Make sure you are getting into a licenced car with a red number plate and P the 1st letter on the registration. Agree a price before you get into the car. Taxis only accept cash and the fare should be quoted in J$.

The southwest

Negril, the main tourist town in the west, earned a reputation in the days of hippies and is still considered more laid back than other destinations. Its seven-mile beach attracts families, couples and students on their spring breaks and accommodation is equally varied, from basic cabins to boutique luxury hotels. Long ignored by all except fisherman, the south coast is gradually attracting attention from visitors. Treasure Beach has a few small hotels, of which Jake's has a number of celebrity devotees, and Sandals has a large resort at Whitehouse. Attractions in the area are numerous and varied, from the crocodiles in Black River to the rum factory at the Appleton Estate.

Negril → *For listings, see pages 80-84.*

Negril, on a seven-mile stretch of pure white sand on the west end of the island, is far less formal than other tourist spots but is still a one-industry town. The town is at the south end of Long Bay; at the north is the smaller Bloody Bay, where whalers used to carve up their catch. Beyond that is Half Moon Bay, a very quiet, peaceful and private beach with hammocks and a beach bar. There are rock pools to explore, snorkelling, kayaking and other water toys. Hotels, holiday homes, fishermen's huts and beach bars straggle the length of Long Bay, also called Seven Mile Beach, with areas of coconut palms and other trees and plants which obscure some of the buildings. The main part of the town has resorts and beaches but no snorkelling and you have to take a boat.

Hawkers ('higglers'), pushing their drugs, hair braiding, aloe, etc, on the beach, are annoying and reported to be worse than at Montego Bay. Politely decline whatever they are offering (if you do not want it). Fruit is readily available although not ready to eat; ask the vendor to cut it up and put it in a bag for you. To avoid the worst of the higglers go to the end of the beach near the crafts market where there are no stalls or bars.

Places in Negril

In the West End of the town are beautiful cliffs and many fine caves, with great snorkelling but no beaches. **Rick's Café** is famous as a spot to watch local youth cliff jumping into the sea. While fun to watch, you may get tired of the pestering for tips for them to do it again. At the far end of West End Road, past the restaurants and boutique hotels, is the **Negril Lighthouse**, built in 1894 and still in operation. In between West End and Seven-Mile Beach is an area with neither beaches nor cliffs. Behind the bay is the **Great Morass**, which is a protected area as a natural wetland.

The **Royal Palm Reserve** ⓘ *T957 3736 (office), T364 7407 (reserve), 0900-1800, birdwatching by appointment from 0600, US$10, children US$5,* is well worth a visit, a little way out of Negril on the south coast road to Sheffield. The **Jamaican Petroleum**

Marine life and diving

Marine life and diving There are marine parks in Montego Bay, Port Antonio, Negril and Ocho Rios. The **Jamaica Protected Areas Trust** website (www.jpat-jm.com) has information on all four, as well as other protected areas on the island. The **Montego Bay Marine Park** ① T9525619, www.mbmp.org, stretches from the east end of the airport to the Great River and contains three major ecosystems: seagrass bed, mangroves and coral reefs. It aims to protect the offshore reef from urban waste, over-fishing and hillside erosion leading to excessive soil deposition. Non-motorized watersports such as diving, snorkelling and glass-bottom boat tours are permitted, but you are not allowed to touch or remove anything. There are several conservation groups involved in marine ecology. The **White River Watershed and Ocho Rios Marine Park Association** ① WHROMP– on Facebook, is a public/private partnership which aims to protect the natural resources and management of the White River watershed and the Ocho Rios Marine Park in a sustainable manner. The **Northern Jamaica Conservation Association** ① NJCA, Sevenoaks, PO Box 212, Runaway Bay, St Ann, on Facebook, and www.n-j-c-a.yolasite.com, actively promotes conservation along the northern coast. Similar is the **Portland Environment Protection Association** ① 6 Allan Ave, Port Antonio, T993 9632, www.pepa-jamaica.org. The **Negril Coral Reef Preservation Society** ① T957 4627, www.negril.com/ncrps,

has installed permanent mooring buoys for recreational boats and works on educational programmes with schools. The Negril marine park set up in conjunction with protected coastal and terrestrial habitats, aims at protecting the coral reefs and improving fish stocks. Jamaica's largest protected area is **Portland Bight** ① PBPA, on the south coast, T986 3344, www.ccam.org.jm, which includes not only the marine environment, but also the surrounding land and the offshore cays.

Around Negril there are many reef sites and a huge variety of marine life: coral, sponges, invertebrates, sea turtles, octopus, starfish and lots of fish. Off Montego Bay and Ocho Rios there is wall diving quite close to shore and a few wrecks. Off Port Antonio fish are attracted to freshwater springs which provide good feeding grounds. The best wreck diving is off Port Royal and Kingston where you can also explore the city that slid into the sea in the 1692 earthquake. You will need a permit and to be escorted if diving the lost city.

Dive centres Nearly all dive operators are based at hotels along the north coast. The **Jamaica Association of Dive Operators** (JADO) offers courses at all levels. Contact the tourist board for a full list of operators and map of dive sites. Diving can be included in a hotel package. A two-tank dive costs on average US$100. Dives are limited to 30 m. There is a hyperbaric chamber at the University of the West Indies' Discovery Bay Marine Laboratory, St Ann.

Corporation mined it for peat in the late 1970s, but they gave up and left the resulting pond and forest for ecological purposes. The reserve, at 289 acres, is part of the 6000-acre wetland protected by the NEPT, on and offshore. Apart from a wonderful collection of palms, you can see the West Indian whistling duck and blue herons on the water, with red tilapia and tarpon in the pond, as well as Jamaican boa and crocodile, which are less visible. The boardwalk and viewing tower have not been well maintained and the place is in sore need of attention, officially closed in 2013, but you can still visit independently. There are guides who can help you understand the ecology of the area and a very good birding guide who will help you spot numerous species including many of the endemics.

Kool Runnings ① *Norman Manley Blvd, opposite Beaches Hotel, T957 5400, www. koolrunnings.com, usually closed Mon, also Sep and much of Oct-Nov, US$75 for waterpark and adventure zone with all activities included, US$33 for water park, lazy river and entry only to adventure zone, US$22 children under 4 ft tall, US$19 after 1500, excluding holidays, under 2s free*, is a water park and adventure zone with amusement and entertainment facilities. The park promises the 'greatest chill' under the sun and there is a variety of chutes and slides, rafting and tubing, a climbing wall, bungee trampolining, go-karting, paintballing, laser kombat, kayaking on the Morass, etc.

By the **Poinciana Beach Resort** is the **Anancy Park** ① *Tue-Sun 1300-2200*, with boating lake, minigolf, go-karts, fishing pond, nature trail, and historical exhibitions.

The **Negril Environmental Protection Trust (NEPT)** ① *Norman Manley Blvd, T957 3115*, is an NGO charged with managing the Negril Environmental Protection Area, which includes a marine park managed by the **Negril Coral Reef Preservation Society (NCRPS)** ① *T957 3735*. The NEPT is spearheading a four-year US$3 million project from 2013 to restore the beach and environment in the Negril area, aimed at the long-term conservation of the Great Morass area. The Negril Morass is drying out and is plagued by fires caused by human activity, including clearing the land for building houses and for farming. The wetland's functions as a filter of pollutants (pesticides and fertilizers damage the reef once they reach the sea) and flood protection have been diminished because of these unsustainable activities and drainage. Ultimately this could threaten the tourist industry, so key stakeholders, including farmers who need to sell their produce to hotels and restaurants, are supporting the scheme to keep the wetland wet.

The south coast → *For listings, see pages 80-84.*

Savanna-la-Mar

About 29 km east of Negril, on the coast, is Savanna-la-Mar, Sav-la-Mar, or just Sav, a busy, commercial town with shopping and banks, but no major attractions for tourists. The town was almost completely destroyed by hurricanes in 1748 and 1780 and had to be rebuilt. It was a key player in the sugar and slave trade until slavery was abolished in 1833, whereupon the freed residents helped many slaves aboard US ships disembark and gain their freedom as soon as they touched British soil. Easily reached by minibus from Negril, there are hourly buses from Montego Bay (US$2). The **Frome sugar refinery**, 8 km north of Savanna-la-Mar, will often allow visitors to tour their facilities during sugar cane season (November-June). The 9.5-km **Roaring River** has a cave where the river flows underground, 3 km north of Petersfield which, although open to the public and being run by the community, has no electric light connected at present. Guides will be happy to charge you US$15 for a 15-minute tour in the dark, lit only by a kerosene flame. You will be told about Taíno occupancy, Obeah rituals, bats and guano, but without decent torches or functioning light bulbs you may well be disappointed. It is a scenic area with interesting walks and streams suitable for bathing.

Bluefields and Belmont

Outside Savanna-la-Mar, the main south coast road (A2) passes by Paradise Plantation, a private estate with miles of frontage on **Bluefields Bay**, a protected anchorage with

Deep-sea fishing

Deep-sea fishing for white marlin, wahoo, tuna and dolphin fish can be arranged at north coast hotels. A half-day charter starts at about US$550, but prices depend on the number of people and the length of trip (three to four hours), plus a 10% tip for the crew, who will expect to keep half the catch. There is a blue marlin tournament at Port Antonio (mid-October) and others at Montego Bay (September or October) and Falmouth (August or September).

reefs and wetlands teeming with birds. At Ferris Crossroads, the A2 meets up with the B8 road, a well-maintained north-south connection and about 40 minutes' drive to Montego Bay via Whithorn and Anchovy. For the next 6.5 km the A2 hugs the coast along the road to Bluefields, where there is a white-sand beach mainly used by locals. There is no mass tourism either in Bluefields or in the adjacent village of Belmont although there are some luxury villas and a **Sandals Resort** at Whitehouse.

The south coast is known as the best part of Jamaica for deep-sea fishing and boat trips go out from Belmont to the reefs or to offshore banks. Snorkelling is also good because the sea is mainly calm in the morning. The **Bluefields Great House**, was the place where Philip Gosse lived in the 1830s and wrote his book, *Birds of Jamaica*. The house is currently in a state of disrepair and empty but the grounds reportedly contain the first breadfruit tree planted in Jamaica by Captain Bligh after his expedition to the South Pacific.

Belmont is visited by reggae fans who come to see the **Peter Tosh Mausoleum**. A guide will show you the guitarist's tomb, memorabilia and the surrounding garden in front of his mother and stepfather's house. He grew up in this area before he went to Trench Town and joined up with Bob Marley and Bunny Wailer and he was a committed Rastafari before his murder in 1987.

Brighton

In Brighton, a growing new attraction is the **Blue Hole Mineral Spring** ① *T860 8805, www.facebook.com/BlueHoleMineralSpringJamaica, US$10*, where there is a 12-m-deep blue hole in the karst limestone you can jump into, swing on a rope and drop into or just swim in by descending an 8-m ladder. Little fish will nibble your dead skin and you can rub mineral salts on your skin and swim through small caves and tunnels. There is also a swimming pool filled with the same water if you don't want to jump, a bar, restaurant and restrooms. The staff are very friendly and helpful, making this a relaxing but fun place to come.

Black River

Black River is one of the oldest towns in Jamaica. It had its heyday in the 18th century when it was the main exporting harbour for logwood dyes. Along the shore are some fine early 19th-century mansions, some of which are being restored. In the town there several lovely old wooden buildings and a yellow brick parish church, low, squat and solid. At Black River, you can go by boat from across the bridge up the lower stretches of the Black River, the second longest river in Jamaica. You should see crocodiles, mostly at midday basking on the river banks, and plenty of birdlife in tranquil surroundings. Some of the boat captains call them over, attracting them with chicken pieces and then catch them for you to touch. This has, of course, completely changed their behaviour as wild creatures.

To avoid large tour parties, go with a local, whose boats are through the fish market. The boats are smaller, slower, quieter and go further up river. They stop at a 'countryside bar' rather than the one the large tour companies use (see Tour operators, page 84). The Black River flows first through the Upper Morass, being joined by other rivers before flowing through the Lower Morass, a huge area of swamp and one of the Caribbean's largest, with great biodiversity.

Treasure Beach

On the south coast past Black River is Treasure Beach, a wide dark-sand beach with body-surfing waves, in one of the most beautiful areas on the island. It is largely used by local fishermen as it is the closest point to the Pedro Banks. There is one small grocery shop and a bakery. A van comes to the village every day with fresh fruit and vegetables. This area is quite unlike any other part of Jamaica and still relatively unvisited by tourists. The local people are very friendly and you will be less hassled by higglers than elsewhere. Frenchman's Beach is the best for swimming, then Calabash Bay. You can take a daytime or moonlight tour to **Sunny Island** (Alligator Reef) from **Jake's Hotel**. Hire a fishing boat to go to **Pelican Bar**, run by Floyd, on a sand bar 1 km out to sea, entirely rebuilt on stilts of timber and thatch after Hurricane Ivan swept through in 2004.

To the east of Treasure Beach lies **Lovers' Leap** ⓘ *T965 6577, daily 1000-1800, there is an entry fee which varies from US$1.50 to US$10 and covers parking and a guided tour*, a beauty spot named after the slave and his lover (his owner's daughter) who jumped off the cliff in despair. Alternatively it is named after two slaves who were about to be separated by their master, who wanted the woman for himself. Take your pick. There is a restaurant and bar and it is a lovely spot to watch the sunset. You are high enough up to see birds flying below you. East of Alligator Pond is **Gut River**, where you can sometimes see alligators and manatees. Boat and fishing trips can be made to **Pigeon Island**, with a day on the island for swimming and snorkelling.

Moving inland → *For listings, see pages 80-84.*

Bamboo Avenue

Inland on the A2 is Middle Quarters, on the edge of the Black River Morass, hot pepper shrimp are sold by the wayside, but make sure they are today's catch. Just after Middle Quarters is the left turn which takes you to **YS Falls** ⓘ *T997 6360, www.ysfalls.com, Tue-Sun 0930-1530, closed public holidays, US$15, children US$7.50, tubing US$6, zip line US$42 and children US$20, 15-min walk from car park*, (pronounced Why-Ess), in the middle of a large private plantation where they produce beef cattle and breed race horses. River bathing is popular with local families as well as tour parties and there are changing rooms and composting toilets. A walkway follows the course of the river and up the tiered falls to the top pool where there is a rope for swinging (gloves provided and life jackets when the river is full). The natural pool, surrounded by decking, is fed by a nearby spring and is always clear even when the river and falls are in full spate. A cool spot for non-swimmers. The restaurant by the entrance is a bit of a trek back for lunch, so take your own picnic if you want to stay by the river. Further along the A2 is the impressive 2½-mile long Bamboo Avenue.

North of Bamboo Avenue is **Maggotty**, on the (closed) railway line from Montego Bay to Kingston and close to the **Appleton Estate** ⓘ *T963 9215, www.appletonrum.com, Mon-Sat 0900-1600, US$25*, where tours of the rum factory are offered and there is good rum tasting. A buffet lunch is offered with advance reservation, vegetarian or other special requirements catered for.

Mandeville

After Bamboo Avenue, the A2 road goes through Lacovia and Santa Cruz, an expanding town on the St Elizabeth Plain, and on up to Mandeville, a peaceful upland town with perhaps the best climate on the island. It is very spread out, with building on all the surrounding hills and no slums. In recent years, Mandeville has derived much of its prosperity from the bauxite/alumina industry (outside the town). There are lots of expensive homes and the town is congested.

The town's centre is the village green, now called **Cecil Charlton Park** (after the ex-mayor, whose opulent mansion, Huntingdon Summit, can be visited by prior arrangement). The green looks a bit like New England; at its northeast side stands a **Georgian courthouse** and, on the southeast, **St Mark's parish church** (both 1820). By St Mark's is the **market** area (busiest days Monday, Wednesday and Friday) and the area where buses congregate. West of the green, at the corner of Ward Avenue and Caledonia Road, is the **Manchester Club** ① *T962 2403*, one of the oldest country clubs in the West Indies (1868) and the oldest in Jamaica. It has a nine-hole golf course (18 tee boxes, enabling you to play 18 holes) and tennis and squash courts (you must be introduced by a member).

Around Mandeville

Although some way inland, Mandeville is a good place from which to start exploring both the surrounding area and the south coast. In fact, by car you can get to most of Jamaica's resorts, except those east of Ocho Rios or Kingston, in two hours or less. Birdwatchers and those interested in seeing a beautiful 'great house' in a cattle-breeding property should contact Ann Sutton at **Marshall's Pen** ① *T904 5454, US$10 for great house tour by appointment only*. The 1795 stone and timber house is square and sturdy with louvred windows. The outbuildings of the former coffee estate have been converted to other uses, including guest cottages for birdwatchers, but you can still see evidence of the old coffee factory. It gets its name from the fact that it was originally a cattle ranch before coffee was grown. It has been in the Sutton family since 1939. Robert Sutton is an ornithologist and co-author, with Audrey Downer and Yves-Jacques Rey-Millet, of Birds of Jamaica: A Photographic Field Guide (Cambridge University Press, 1990). More than 100 bird species have been seen on the estate, including 25 of the endemics. An archaeology project is ongoing to investigate the slave village occupied between 1812 and 1838 when the freed slaves were moved to a free township nearby, see Facebook. Also around the town by prior reservation, you can visit the small **High Mountain Coffee** ① *Main Rd, Williamsfield, T963 4211, Mon-Fri, 1000-1600, free*, **Pioneer Chocolate Company** ① *Williamsfield, T963 4216*, the Alcan works, and local gardens.

From Mandeville it is about 88.5 km east to Kingston on the A2, bypassing May Pen, through Old Harbour then on to Spanish Town and Kingston. Before the May Pen bypass, a road branches south to **Milk River Bath** ① *May Pen, Clarendon, T610 7745/924 9544, milkriverhotel@yahoo.com, daily 0700-2100, US$2, 15 mins, restaurant and hotel*, the world's most radioactive spa. Owned by the government since it opened in 1796, the baths are somewhat run-down, but the medical properties of the water are among the best. Five kilometres from the baths is **Alligator Hole**, part of the Canoe Valley National Nature Preserve, which stretches west to Alligator Pond. At Alligator Hole three rescued manatees may be seen.

The southwest listings

For hotel and restaurant price codes and other relevant information, see pages 12-14.

🛏 Where to stay

Negril *p74*

$$$$ The Caves Hotel & Spa, Lighthouse Rd, West End, T957 0270, www.islandout post.com. All-inclusive luxury, 12 1-bedroom and 2-bedroom suites and cottages and a 4-bedroom villa, all different with lots of privacy, no children under 16. Lots of private areas on the cliffs with sundecks, little nooks, steps down to the sea through limestone rock. Private dining room in cave lit by candles for romantic dining. Sauna and massage, spa with sea view.

$$$$ Sunset at the Palms, Norman Manley Blvd, on Bloody Bay, across the road from the beach, T957 5350, www.sunsetatthe palms.com. All-inclusive, deluxe rooms and suites in wooden cabins on stilts, rustic elegance, light and airy, Asian-inspired furnishings, wonderful showers, pool, swim-up bar, private beach, tennis, restaurants, fruit from the 10-acre garden, piano bar, adults only, security guards keep away 'higglers'.

$$$$-$$$ Banana Shout Resort, West End Rd, T957 0384, www.bananashout resort.com. 4 colourful wooden cottages with kitchenettes on the cliffs with a ladder for access to a private cove and the sea. Hammocks and verandas for good sunset watching. A small bar in the garden for guests only serves breakfast lunch and dinner.

$$$$-$$$ Charela Inn, Norman Manley Blvd, on the beach, T957 4648, www.charela.com. 47 rooms around pool, access for wheelchairs, 3 rooms for the less able, family-owned and run, wide beach, kayaks, sunfish, sailboards, restaurant, bar, meal plans, French chef, wine brought from France, own bakery on site, old-fashioned dining room, dress code for dinner.

$$$$-$$$ Firefly Beach Cottages, Long Bay, on the beach and therefore not very private, T957 4358, www.jamaicalink.com. From a basic cabin for 2 or studios, to 1- to 3-bedroomed cottages or villas, clothes optional, old-fashioned furniture, rather cramped, breakfast available but no restaurant on site.

$$$$-$$$ Negril Escape Resort and Spa, West End, T957 0393, www.negril escape.com. On cliffs, rooms and apartments, yoga, spa, PADI and NAUI instructors for diving at Negril Scuba Centre on site or at the Boardwalk Village, to where there is a regular beach shuttle.

$$$$-$$$ Rockhouse, Lighthouse Rd, T957 4373, www.rockhousehotel.com. On cliffs at Pristine Cove, just north of **Rick's Café**, 34 a/c rooms by the sea in studios or villas built of timber, stone and thatch, cliff-edge pool, romantic restaurant above the water serving 'new Jamaican cuisine', no beach but steps down to sea, snorkelling and yoga, quiet, restful, Australian-owned, no children under 12 because of potentially dangerous cliffs.

$$$$-$$$ Rondel Village, Norman Manley Blvd, T957 4413, www.rondelvillage.com. 56 rooms in 1-3 bedroom villas on 3 floors, some have jacuzzis off master bedroom, all have TV, fridge, a/c, fan, light, bright colours but a bit cramped with a lot of rooms in a small lot. Irie beach restaurant and bar, good bit of beach, plenty of sand, sun beds. Garden rooms across the road are cheaper.

$$$$-$$$ Seasplash, Norman Manley Blvd, T957 4041, www.seasplash.com. Rooms and suites, some with kitchenettes, very good value in summer, spacious, comfortable, good fittings and furnishings, everything you could need and on the beach with a good restaurant on site: **Norma's on the Beach**.

$$$$-$$$ Tensing Pen, Lighthouse Rd, West End, T957 0387, www.tensingpen.com. Well-established upmarket hotel but unpretentious and sociable. Rooms, suites and cottages in lush, leafy gardens, some adjoining can be suites, rooms on stilts with open showers downstairs, no a/c, no TV, supremely relaxing, breakfast included 0730-1100. All the advantages of a hotel but with the independence of a villa. Yoga hut, massage, hammocks, lots of private areas for sunbathing.

$$$ Banana's Garden, West End Rd, opposite **Rick's Café**, T957 0909, www.bananasgarden.com. 5 sweet little cottages in gorgeous garden with pool. A friendly, quiet, relaxing bed & breakfast, massages available, very family oriented.

$$$-$$ Alvynegril Guesthouse, One Love Dr, West End Rd, no phone, www.alvy negril.com. 5 rooms, 4 with twin beds and 1 queen, all with a/c, fridge, tea/coffee, sea view, perched on top of cliffs above caves where catamarans come for snorkelling trips. Jump in, swim through the caves and come up ladder into Aunt Mae's garden across the street. Very friendly and safe, good for lone travellers, couples or families. Lots of restaurants and bars nearby.

Bluefields and Belmont *p76*
$$$$ Bluefields Bay Jamaica Villas, Bluefields Bay, T877-955 8993, www. bluefieldsvillas.com. 6 luxury villas with 2-6 bedrooms on the shore, all-inclusive with every service imaginable, concierge, chef, housekeeper, nanny, good for romantic couples or family gatherings.

$$-$ Nature Roots, Belmont, T955 8162. The owner, Brian, is a Rastafari and organic farmer. He has a 2-bedroom cottage to rent with kitchen and living room, in a banana grove, and a cottage with 4 simple rooms to rent with shared kitchen and bathroom. Discounts for long stays. His wife can cook traditional Jamaican meals for you. This is real Jamaica living and you'll get to know all the neighbours: woodcarvers, farmers, fishermen, taxi drivers.

Black River *p77*
$$$ Ashton Great House, up hillside, Luana, just outside Black River to the west, T965 2036. Lovely old plantation house with balconies and fretwork detail. Pool, huge, traditional Jamaican breakfast, other meals available, 24 rooms, very quiet.

$$-$ Waterloo Guest House, 44 High St, T965 2278. A Georgian building, the first house in Jamaica with electric light. Beside the sea and in walking distance of the town. Old rooms in the main house are no longer used, needing renovation, so guests are put in the new annex at the back, all with showers and a/c, good restaurant (lobster in season).

Treasure Beach *p78*
$$$$-$$$ Jake's, Calabash Bay, T965 0635, www.jakeshotel.com. Run by award-winning Jason Henzell. One of the loveliest places to stay in the Caribbean. Intimate, friendly, a great place. Rustic rooms in small, brightly painted cottages, all different with themed designs. Also honeymoon suites in individual buildings on the shore, like iced cakes in pretty blue or pink with rooftop sun deck where you can have room service. Or there are villas with 2-6 bedrooms. Games room/library with TV/VCR, **Dougie's** bar by salt water pool looking out to sea. Boat trips, riding, cycling and hiking can be arranged, yoga and massage, music. 2 restaurants, very good food, lovely banana pancakes for breakfast.

$$$$-$$$ Sunset Resort, Treasure Beach next to **Jake's**, T965 0143, www.sunset resort.com. Rooms and suites, flexible accommodation, Jamaican decor, good for family groups, view from cliff top down to beach with fishing boats and pelicans, US and Jamaican owned, lots of flags, keen fisherman, Astroturf around the pool. Bar and restaurant, unlimited buffet Fri night.

Mandeville *p79*
$$$ Mandeville Hotel, 4 Hotel St, T962 2460, www.mandevillehotel.com. Spacious,

pool, excursions arranged, good staff but tired hotel and poor food.

Around Mandeville *p79*
$$ Kariba Kariba, Atkinson's Dr, near New Green roundabout on Winston Jones highway, 1st right off New Green Rd, 45 mins' walk from centre, on bus route, T962 8006. Bath, fan, 5 large rooms or suites, small breakfast included, TV lounge, bar, dining room. The owners, Derrick and Hazel O'Conner, are friendly, knowledgeable and hospitable, they can arrange for you to meet local people with similar interests and offer tours. Derrick is developing a 5-ha farm at Mile Gully and plans to develop a small campsite, bar, accommodation and other facilities there.

⊕ Restaurants

Negril *p74*
Eating cheaply is difficult but not impossible. The native restaurant-food stalls are good and relatively cheap; the local patties are delicious. Street hawkers will sell you jerk chicken.
$$$ Norma's, at **Seasplash** hotel, see above, T957 4041. Breakfast, lunch and dinner. On decking with steps down to sea, by pool and bar, sun beds on narrow strip of sand. Very good food, smoked marlin a speciality for any meal.
$$$ Office of Nature, Bloody Bay on the beach. Open 24 hrs. Good, fresh lobster, straight out of the sea for US$25 served with a cold Red Stripe for US$2.50, friendly service, rustic bar, a good place to meet the locals.
$$$-$$ Hungry Lion, Lighthouse Rd, West End, T957 4486. Open 1100-2300, Sat until 0200. Small, colourful and arty crafty, art on the walls, gift shop. Lunch downstairs in lounge-style restaurant, dinner upstairs on roof terrace or indoors, open from 1700, healthy eating, natural foods, salads, sandwiches, fish for lunch, crab backs, shrimp, vegetarian options, pasta for dinner. Bar and occasional night-time entertainment with screen for showing unusual DVDs and documentaries.

$$$-$$ Murphy's, Lighthouse Rd, West End, just past Rick's Café, T367 0475, see Facebook. Casual bar and restaurant, great host and chef, all-day breakfast, jerk chicken and seafood, including lobster. Pay in J$ as exchange rate is poor.
$$$-$$ Rick's Café, T457 0380. Lunch 1200-1600, dinner and entertainment 1800-2200. Full ocean view from clifftop setting, famous for the local divers who throw themselves off the rocks and trees into the sea for tips. Food ranges from surf'n'turf down to coco bread chips and salsa dip, Cuban and Jamaican cigars, live music in evenings on small stage, lively place and a must for a sunset drink.
$$$-$$ Sun Beach, Norman Manley Blvd, south of Margaritaville, T957 9118. Open 0730-2200, later at weekends. Restaurant and bar on beach, sunbeds on sand, snacks and salads, fish, ginger curry chicken, sauteed snapper, 2-for-1 lobster special Sun nights, live music on Sun.
$$ Cosmos, on the beach, north of **Sandals Beaches**, T957 4330. Open 0900-2200, food from 1100. Wide area of sand under palm trees, seating at benches on sand or at tables under roof by bar. Local food at reasonable prices, popular, red pea soup, curry goat, stews, fish, conch, with local accompaniments, rice and peas, steamed or fried bammy, hearty and filling.

Black River *p77*
$$$-$$ Fish Pot Bistro, on the river by the boats, T965 2211. Lunch and dinner (mosquitoes at dusk), serving fish, lobster, garlic crab. Also pizza.
$$ Bayside, 17 High St, near bridge, T965 2537. Excellent steamed fish with rice and peas, usually all gone by 1300. Jerk and barbecue section at the back over the water.

Treasure Beach *p78*
$$$-$$ Little Ochie, Alligator Pond, on the beach, T382 3375, www.littleochie. com. Open 1100-2300, later at weekends, depending on customers. Blackie's fish restaurant is legendary, everything freshly

caught, sit at wooden tables under thatch, some made out of old fishing boats with benches for tables, raised on stilts above the sand. Choose your fish, shrimp, lobster or crab from the fridge and they'll cook it however you want, very fresh and tasty, garnished with spicy onion (pickled), carrot and scotch bonnet chillies, accompanied by festival or bammy. Watch out for unposted prices though as there is no menu.

Mandeville *p79*
$$$ Bloomfield Great House, 8 Perth Rd, T962 7130, bloomfield.g.h@cwjamaica.com. Originally a coffee estate, part of its land was used to build the town, 200 m above Mandeville, panoramic views. The Georgian great house has also been used as a hotel, a dairy, a private home and more recently, **Bill Laurie's Steak House**, now owned by Ralph Pearce (Australian) and his wife Pamela Grant (Jamaican). Open for lunch and dinner, varied menu, fish 'n' chips, filet mignon, beer-batter shrimp, home-made pasta, smoked marlin, cheesecakes are a speciality.

Bars and clubs

Negril *p74*
Live reggae shows in outdoor venues most nights, featuring local and well-known stars. Entrance is usually US$5-10, good fun, lively atmosphere, very popular. Nice bars are located along the beach, usually with music. For beautiful surroundings try any of the bars at the hotels on the cliffs on the West End Rd, where there is great sunset watching to go with great cocktails.
Alfred's, Norman Manley Blvd, T957 4669, www.alfreds.com. Nightly entertainment, live music, varied programme, reggae Tue, Fri, Sun, on the beach, open air. Also bar, restaurant and guesthouse.
The Jungle, Norman Manley Blvd, across from **Rondel Village**, T957 3283, www.junglenegril.com. Daily from 2200 until dawn, queues start at 1100, gets going 2400, noise abatement rules kick in at 0200

but club doesn't close until 0400-0430. Entry depending on night. Used to be a bank and still looks like it, with vault doors. Ladies' Night Thu when women enter for free and men pay US$10, Dancehall Night Fri, restaurant and bar, lots of high spirits, gaming room open from 1500 until the club closes, sports bar, pool tables, ATM, snacks and stage for comedy and other entertainment, occasionally live music, but mostly DJs. Plenty of security on gate, vendors outside to increase traffic jam.
Roots Bamboo, Norman Manley Blvd, T957 4479, www.rootsbamboobeach.com. The place to come on Wed night when they have a live reggae band playing and you can dance on the sand. Good mix of locals and foreigners.

Treasure Beach *p78*
Floyde's Pelican Bar, 30 mins out to sea on a sandbank. Reached by fishing boat, US$20 round trip, Floyde Forbes' bar is built of wood and thatched with palm fronds, a precarious stilted construction furnished with mismatched wooden tables and bench seating, while underneath hover sting rays waiting for scraps and pelicans sit on the roof. Floyde will cook fish and rice, whatever he has caught that day, and serve up drinks from a cooler. Tours of the Black River sometimes stop by for daytime drinks, while guests at **Jake's** come out at sunset or for a full moon.

Shopping

Negril *p74*
The **Craft Market** is overwhelming, with 200 stalls of sarongs and wood carvings, not much in the way of variety and everyone wants your attention.

What to do

Negril *p74*
Diving
Marine Life Divers, Samsara Hotel, West End, T957 3245, www.mldiversnegril.com.

Boat and shore diving, cliff diving, full range of courses in English and German. **Sundivers**, a PADI 5-star facility close to the roundabout in Negril square at **Travellers Beach Resort**, T957 4503, www.sundiversnegril.com. Free pick-up, full range of courses and equipment rental, also snorkelling, glass bottom boat tours and sunset cruises.

Golf
Tryall Golf, Tennis and Beach Resort, Sandy Bay, between Montego Bay and Negril, T956 5660/81, www.tryallclub.com/golf-at-tryall/pro-shop. Par 71, 6328 m in 890-ha resort complex, probably the best known with a Golf Academy and hosts the annual **Johnny Walker Pro Am Championship**. Advance bookings are essential.
Negril Hills Golf Club, Sheffield, inland, up in the hills near Negril, T957 4638, www.negrilhillsgolfclub.com. Par 72, 5790 m, 18-hole course with clubhouse, restaurant, pro shop and tennis.

Road races
The Reggae marathon and half marathon for runners and walkers, www.reggae marathon.com. An annual event in Dec, starting at 0515. Well-supported marathon and half marathon, begins and ends at Long Bay Beach Park.

Black River p77
Tour operators
Charles Swaby's South Coast Safaris, 1 Crane Rd in Black River, T965 2513. Takes up to 250 people per tour, looking for crocodiles, 1½ hrs, 5 times a day, from east side of Black River bridge.
Irie Safari, 12 High St, T634 4232, lintonirie@ hotmail.com. Takes a maximum of 35 passengers twice a day, using several different sizes of boat, wheelchair access. The captain is a guide, giving a rounded tour, educational, not just watching

crocodiles but spotting birds and crabs and other wetland creatures. The owner, Lloyd Linton, is a wetland biologist and also runs **Lost River Kayak Adventures**, offering kayaking tours upriver beyond the crocodiles to the fresh water where there are blue holes for swimming and lots of birds. Fishing trips for tarpon and snook also arranged.

Mandeville p79
Golf
Manchester Club, Wint Rd, T962 2403. 9-holes, also tennis and squash.

Road races
High Mountain Coffee, www.high mountaincoffee10k.com. 1 of several races during the year. 10-km and 5-km races and 5-km walk at Williamsfield, Manchester, in Jan, which usually attract around 450 runners.

⊖ Transport

Negril p74
Licensed, unmetered taxis have red licence plates with PP before the numbers. Avoid unlicensed taxis. Route taxis charge less for locals than for tourists. A taxi will cost US$5 plus tip into town from the beach hotels or from the cliffs, but US$10 from the cliffs to the beach. Local buses operate between Negril and Montego Bay stopping frequently.
JUTA Tours, Norman Manley Blvd, T957 4620, www.jutatoursnegrilltd.com, offer transfers by bus, van or taxi from the **Donald Sangster Airport**, **Montego Bay** to Negril. Taxis charge about US$65-70 one way for 1-3 people. Most of the Negril all-inclusive hotels arrange free transport for you, and other hotels will offer transfers for US$25-30 per person, but it can be time-consuming while you drop off or pick up guests at other hotels along the way. Lots of companies do bike rental.

Contents

Footnotes

Index

Titles available in the Footprint *Focus* range

Latin America	UK RRP	US RRP
Bahia & Salvador	£7.99	$11.95
Brazilian Amazon	£7.99	$11.95
Brazilian Pantanal	£6.99	$9.95
Buenos Aires & Pampas	£7.99	$11.95
Cartagena & Caribbean Coast	£7.99	$11.95
Costa Rica	£8.99	$12.95
Cuzco, La Paz & Lake Titicaca	£8.99	$12.95
El Salvador	£5.99	$8.95
Guadalajara & Pacific Coast	£6.99	$9.95
Guatemala	£8.99	$12.95
Guyana, Guyane & Suriname	£5.99	$8.95
Havana	£6.99	$9.95
Honduras	£7.99	$11.95
Nicaragua	£7.99	$11.95
Northeast Argentina & Uruguay	£8.99	$12.95
Paraguay	£5.99	$8.95
Quito & Galápagos Islands	£7.99	$11.95
Recife & Northeast Brazil	£7.99	$11.95
Rio de Janeiro	£8.99	$12.95
São Paulo	£5.99	$8.95
Uruguay	£6.99	$9.95
Venezuela	£8.99	$12.95
Yucatán Peninsula	£6.99	$9.95

Asia	UK RRP	US RRP
Angkor Wat	£5.99	$8.95
Bali & Lombok	£8.99	$12.95
Chennai & Tamil Nadu	£8.99	$12.95
Chiang Mai & Northern Thailand	£7.99	$11.95
Goa	£6.99	$9.95
Gulf of Thailand	£8.99	$12.95
Hanoi & Northern Vietnam	£8.99	$12.95
Ho Chi Minh City & Mekong Delta	£7.99	$11.95
Java	£7.99	$11.95
Kerala	£7.99	$11.95
Kolkata & West Bengal	£5.99	$8.95
Mumbai & Gujarat	£8.99	$12.95

Africa & Middle East	UK RRP	US RRP
Beirut	£6.99	$9.95
Cairo & Nile Delta	£8.99	$12.95
Damascus	£5.99	$8.95
Durban & KwaZulu Natal	£8.99	$12.95
Fès & Northern Morocco	£8.99	$12.95
Jerusalem	£8.99	$12.95
Johannesburg & Kruger National Park	£7.99	$11.95
Kenya's Beaches	£8.99	$12.95
Kilimanjaro & Northern Tanzania	£8.99	$12.95
Luxor to Aswan	£8.99	$12.95
Nairobi & Rift Valley	£7.99	$11.95
Red Sea & Sinai	£7.99	$11.95
Zanzibar & Pemba	£7.99	$11.95

Europe	UK RRP	US RRP
Bilbao & Basque Region	£6.99	$9.95
Brittany West Coast	£7.99	$11.95
Cádiz & Costa de la Luz	£6.99	$9.95
Granada & Sierra Nevada	£6.99	$9.95
Languedoc: Carcassonne to Montpellier	£7.99	$11.95
Málaga	£5.99	$8.95
Marseille & Western Provence	£7.99	$11.95
Orkney & Shetland Islands	£5.99	$8.95
Santander & Picos de Europa	£7.99	$11.95
Sardinia: Alghero & the North	£7.99	$11.95
Sardinia: Cagliari & the South	£7.99	$11.95
Seville	£5.99	$8.95
Sicily: Palermo & the Northwest	£7.99	$11.95
Sicily: Catania & the Southeast	£7.99	$11.95
Siena & Southern Tuscany	£7.99	$11.95
Sorrento, Capri & Amalfi Coast	£6.99	$9.95
Skye & Outer Hebrides	£6.99	$9.95
Verona & Lake Garda	£7.99	$11.95

North America	UK RRP	US RRP
Vancouver & Rockies	£8.99	$12.95

Australasia	UK RRP	US RRP
Brisbane & Queensland	£8.99	$12.95
Perth	£7.99	$11.95

For the latest books, e-books and a wealth of travel information, visit us at:
www.footprinttravelguides.com

 footprinttravelguides.com

 Join us on facebook for the latest travel news, product releases, offers and amazing competitions:
www.facebook.com/footprintbooks.